Hey, Kidz!
Buy This Book

Hey, Kidz! Buy This Book

A Radical Primer on Corporate and Governmental Propaganda and Artistic Activism for Short People

Anne Elizabeth Moore

©2004 Anne Elizabeth Moore
Illustrations and Cover Art ©2004 Megan Kelso

Book Design by Nick Stone

Published by Soft Skull Press
www.softskull.com

Distributed by Publishers Group West
www.pgw.com • 800 788 3123

Cataloging in Publication information for this
book is available from the Library of Congress

ISBN 1-932360-35-2

This is written for everyone who ever kept quiet because they thought no one would listen to them. Now, never do that again.

Also, this book is for Princess Kali. She never keeps quiet about anything, but she still deserves a book dedication, a zillion dollars, and her own TV station.

Contents

PREFACE

Shortly after starting this book, I learned of a fourteen-year-old boy in my home state who lit himself on fire while conducting a school project about how media affects youth. Copying a stunt from MTV's *Jackass* for a media studies assignment, the Minnesota boy covered himself with mineral spirits, gazed into the lens of a video camera, warned viewers "Don't try this at home," and sparked a lighter. He covered over 65 percent of his body with third-degree burns and had three major surgeries. He was, however, expected to survive his project about how media affects youth. (The *St. Paul Pioneer Press*, which broke the story, never reported the boy's name in order, they stated, to protect him from the media.)

Of course, I didn't see this news item on TV—certainly not on MTV, and definitely not on *Jackass*. The show would never take responsibility or offer condolences for the boy's physical damage because that wouldn't fit the show's theme of jackassiness. The station would not mention the incident because it wouldn't fit MTV's theme of sexy, rock-and-roll rebelliousness, and the story wouldn't get much TV play because TV itself was partially at fault. This was unfortunate: this boy made a clear and resounding statement about how the media affects youth, but individual programs and the entire medium of television, in refusing to mention it, wouldn't allow his statement to affect the media.

I read about this Midwestern boy in the April 19, 2003, *Billings Gazette* while traveling home to Seattle after working with an afterschool arts and mentorship program in Chicago founded on the principles of Patience, Encouragement, Arts, Consistency, and Hope called the PEACH Club. At the PEACH Club, we worked on a different kind of project about how media affects youth. Everyone—kids *and* adults—in the program made a zine as a way of responding to media representations of youth culture. (Thanks for letting me barge in and hang out for a week, PEACH Club.) The zines we created and the Minnesota boy's video made the same basic point: the media, including television, radio, Internet, newspapers, magazines, and even books, influence us in negative ways. We don't like this influence. It is harmful.

The statement made in the boy's video, however, was much more effective than our zines. He was recreating a "human barbecue" stunt in which a guy in a fireproof suit covers himself in meat and climbs onto a grill. As countless papers reported, he even repeated the warning given before TV stunts when he told people not to try his stunt at home. Unfortunately, he *was* trying it at home and it *was* extremely dangerous. It nearly killed him. The message in his video (which I have not seen and do not wish to see) that we didn't point out in our zines—the message he didn't mean to convey, as it damaged him so severely—is that the media lie blatantly, and they can be more harmful than we realize.

This was his only mistake: in recreating something he had witnessed on television, he allowed the media to come into his life unmediated. Without knowing it, this Midwestern boy permitted a whole array of damaging influences entrance to his life; influences he didn't even know existed. Corporate media interests, advertising propaganda, governmental PR. He claimed, however, to "get it." Ha-ha. He thought he was in on the prank. "Don't try this at home," he inside-joked, knowing his viewers, presumably early teens themselves, would "get it" too. Ha-ha, they would have laughed, had the stunt proceeded as the boy intended, as he had been promised by television it would. His video would have been infamous in that Minnesota high school. It would have made his reputation until graduation. But the stunt did not proceed as the boy had seen it on TV, because no matter how many times we hear the phrase "reality television," the two concepts are not interchangeable. The way things work on television is not the way they work in reality. That is one of the media's biggest and most damaging lies: that television *could* be true. Ha-*ha*, you can almost hear MTV, the inventor of reality television, responding.

TV is particularly deceptive. TV may tell you not to do something, but then show you how to do the thing you're not supposed to do. Given the number of conflicting messages we all process to make sense of TV, it is understandable that this boy might have become confused. He said, "Don't try this at home," implying he was about to do something usually dangerous but that he was safe from, while doing exactly that, trying something dangerous at home. The media (TV, radio, Internet, print, film, and all the corporations behind them) constantly convey untruths, biased opinions, and pointless trivia. This stream of confusing messages by itself shouldn't be able to harm you, but the boy in Minnesota proved that it can.

The media remain our primary sources for information about the world. We learn about romance from Hollywood films, about happy families and healthy bodies from TV commercials, about what's cool from pop radio, about communication from the Internet, and about fear from newspapers. The lesson the boy in Minnesota can teach us is that we need to find a better way of using this information besides emulating it in our daily lives. We need to know more about the people who create our media. We need to understand how they operate and what they want. We need to be able to affect their work. And we need to realize the strength of their sway. The media have been a vital influence on our culture for some time; it is now becoming vital—to kids like the boy in Minnesota—that we interfere with this influence. We must find a way to mediate our media.

This book will show you how. First, I'll tell you a few secrets about the media that most kids don't know. (You'll have to help spread the word.) Then you'll learn how the media trick you. (I'll try to help you trick them as payback.) We'll discuss who controls the media and how, and we'll figure out how this allows politics to be controlled as well. Then we'll talk about making your own media and acting on your own politics. Finally, the resources section, called ways and means, will give you tools to start changing the world to make it better for you. At the end of each chapter, there's an activity called "Try This at Home." They're not physically dangerous activities, but they aren't exactly "safe," either. Be careful. Don't start trouble you can't finish. Since I'm not on MTV's *Jackass*, or MTV's anything, I hope you'll know I'm not lying to you about the danger, but that is up to you to decide.

In the first chapter of this book, we learn the Rule of Logos, which helps us remember that repeating brand names is always advertising. Unfortunately, I sometimes repeat brand names in this book so you can apply the concepts to real-life brands. I don't endorse or use the products I mention, and I hope no one buys them because they think I do. That would really bum me out.

When I don't use real brand names, I make up fake products that do not actually exist, like Smello™, the Fasty-Drive™, and Cutie Snugglefarb™. These fake products can be identified by the little "TM" next to the name. I haven't actually trademarked these products because, like I said, they don't actually exist. These products are too dumb to trademark. If any company takes these ideas, makes them into actual products, and trademarks them, they will be sorry, because they really are very dumb.

This book should be read as a combination of words and pictures. If you don't like reading, everything you need to know can be found in the illustrations. If you don't like pictures, you might be kind of weird. You should learn to like pictures or you will miss out on the best part of this book. Working with illustrator Megan Kelso was a truly collaborative process; I hope everyone can find someone this cool to work with.

I received help on this project from my harshest critics Cake and Thurber, who think I don't take enough naps. Throughout the U.S., I've worked with gazillions of helpful short people, although they probably don't realize how important they are. The Zine Archive and Publishing Project was an amazing resource; I owe much of my current thinking on zines to my work there. Nancy J. Arms Simon reigns as the queen of pie, Tizzy Asher made funny jokes, Nancy Davidson kept me on target, Jeff Henry *can* design his way out of a paper bag, Bee Lavender deserves a party for her contribution to this project, Katherine H. Patterson remains a tireless social service worker and hooker (the rugby kind), and Mina was fantastically helpful in areas of import, including hair-color decisions and paperdoll-making. If this book is weighted toward incredibly smart and talented thirteen-year-old girls, it is due to her influence. Feel free to write to her in care of this book to complain. Genius editor and publisher Richard Nash, who had the original idea for this book, thankfully dropped it into my lap. How I ever lucked out I do not know. Special funding for this project donated by my mom. Kid-tested, mother-approved: my mom. Available wherever mothers are sold. Run right out and get one of my moms today. Hurry! You don't want to miss this opportunity.

Hey, Kidz!
Buy This Book

1. Logoz Rule!

Hey *kidz*! Put down that remote and step away from that magazine! Turn down the radio and get off the Internet! For goodness' sake, stop doing your homework! I gotta tell you a secret!

Move closer to this book for a second. That's it!

Now listen carefully: every time you see a logo or hear a brand name, you're seeing or hearing an advertisement. A logo is an image associated with a particular product, like a visual nickname for a company. Brand names are what corporations rename regular objects to make them seem special. When you spot a logo or a brand name on *anything*, it means a company paid to use that space. Usually, paying someone for space or time to promote a product is called advertising. Sometimes it's called "sponsorship," "product placement," or "endorsement," but here let's call it advertising.

If you're seeing or hearing an advertisement every time you see a logo or hear a brand name, you're taking in a *lot* of ads. First, let's talk about how we take in so much advertising, and then we'll spend the rest of this book figuring out what we can do about it.

Sometimes it's easy to spot advertising. You see ads on TV, and neon signs, billboards, and posters fill our public spaces. In magazines and newspapers, entire pages are devoted to listing the virtues of, and showing people's excitement over, certain products. You can catch commercials on the radio, where they are loud and brash and exciting. On the Internet, advertising can be found in flashing banner ads and pop-up windows. Some websites aimed at youth mark advertising with a character or phrase that appears when you view an ad. Advertising can also be easy to spot in magazine content labeled "advertorial" or on TV shows called "paid programming." Both of these phrases mean the company that created the product also created the content of the show or text of the article.

Even though some of these forms of advertising are difficult to spot, there are many more forms—aimed especially at you—that are even harder to identify.

And they work. Studies show that a lot of kids *don't know* when they're looking at ads or when they're looking at regular TV programming, magazine content, or radio shows. I want to make it easy for you so you can explain it to all your friends: *every time you see a logo or hear a brand name, you're seeing or hearing an advertisement.* Let's call this the Rule of Logos. The Rule of Logos means there are secret ways of advertising that not everyone knows about; that's why it is important to look for a logo or listen for a brand name to decide if you are experiencing an ad.

Apply the Rule of Logos when you watch a movie. If one of the characters drinks a recognizable kind of soft drink (like Diet Coke) while driving a specific kind of car (Ford Focus), to a certain restaurant (maybe the Olive Garden) or store (Toys "R" Us), you'll know it's an ad. This sort of advertising is called "product placement." The creators of the movie were paid to use those specific brands. (By the way, this is not usually true in books. I didn't get any money from these companies, even though I am giving them free advertising when I use their brand names. Usually, I wouldn't mention brand names, but I want you to be aware I'm talking about real things in our culture and not boring, abstract concepts.) On the radio listen for brand names, even if the DJ or reporter is only talking about something cool she ate for dinner last night. If a brand name is mentioned, the DJ was paid to mention it, or given free samples, related services, or nice gifts in exchange for saying the brand name. These are forms of payment in exchange for product promotion. According to the Rule of Logos, that's an advertisement.

This is Not an Advertisement for Fasty-Drive Motor Vehicles

Although the Fasty-Drive™ is the hottest selling item of its class on the market, and clearly the best such item available in its price range, we would not insult you by placing an advertisement in this publication. You are probably too smart for advertising anyway, since you like to read books and stuff. Fasty-Drive™ Motor Vehicle owners are smart like that. They know a good, affordable motor vehicle when they see one. The surprisingly cheap Fasty-Drive™, in fact, is surprisingly cheap, considering how expensive similar products are, and it always smells fresh and clean like a spring breeze. Users of the Fasty-Drive™ feel superior to users of other models, and are also privy to an everlasting sense of euphoria. Also, it is very useful, like for driving from one place to another. (And back!) Kidz, especially, like the Fasty-Drive™ Motor Vehicle because it makes them popular with the attractive sex in their classes at school and raises grade-point averages without studying. When you want to be sure to have fun for the rest of your life, Just Look For the Fasty-Drive™ Logo.

This has been a political announcement paid for by Friends of Fasty-Drive™, a grassroots consumer awareness organization. [See "Having Fun," p. 129]

You'll also see logos printed very small on games. In magazines for youth, advertisers like to make print ads look like mazes or puzzles. They know as well as you do that regular ads are a snore. Some companies make toys to give away for free or very cheap; sometimes those toys are direct replications of products or entire advertisements (does a plastic fast-food meal or teeny pair of plastic designer jeans seem fun to you?). Web ads often are designed to look like computer games. (This could be one of the reasons children eleven and under click on banner ads twice as much as any other age group, as *Ecommerce Times* reported.) Whenever a logo appears on a game or toy, you can be sure that someone paid money to put it there, hoping you would grow to like their brand more.

The Rule of Logos even applies in public schools. Companies provide free posters, free textbook covers, free science experiment kits, free videos, and free equipment to schools in exchange for the advertising value of logos. Do the bathrooms in your school have ads in them? Are there Coke machines in the hallways? Do you use kits in your science or health classes that ask you to test the thickness of name-brand spaghetti sauces, compare nuclear power to solar energy, or discuss the health merits of candy bars, frozen peas, or fast food? Do you participate in projects where you are asked to build things with Legos, to sing commercial jingles about Oscar Meyer Wieners on videotape, or to create art out of donated Pringles cans? Does your sports team scoreboard have a logo on it, or does it flash advertisements for soda, local banks, and athletic equipment? Do you get textbook covers with inspirational and catchy messages on them, like "Just Do It," "Have It Your Way," or "Kid Tested—Mother Approved!"? Does your school collect Campbell's Soup can labels, Orville Redenbacher box tops, or Yoplait yogurt lids? Do you watch Channel One every morning? Do you get free stuff like Always with Wings or Clearasil or Sure deodorant or Crest toothpaste? All of these are little advertisements. "Gifts" like these put logos and brand names in front of you and your friends all day long. "There are only two ways to increase customers," children's marketing consultant Dr. James McNeal told *Child Magazine* for the article "KIDS: The New Captive Market." "Either you switch them to your brand or you grow them from birth. Schools are targeted [with ads] because that's where children are."

Outside of school, you may see these same advertisements at the library or gym, in the science or art museum, at the aquarium, or wherever you hang out. Some restaurants give away free meals to kids on their birthdays so kids will think of the restaurant fondly. Entire fads have been invented and perpetuated by advertising: Pogs, the Pet Rock, Yu-Gi-Oh cards. These things are only desirable because advertisements describe how to use them: they don't *do* anything interesting on their own. Sometimes, companies create entirely new holidays to promote their products. Try to find their logos wherever you see posters announcing the new holiday. Be wary of celebrations like Beef Month (sponsored by the American Beef Council) or Give-Your-Brother-A-Schwinn Day. These holidays urge you to purchase certain goods. Big companies pay millions of dollars to have a float in Macy's Thanksgiving Day Parade or sponsor a ride at Disneyland. Wherever you go and whatever you do, even just for fun, logos and brand names are there. Even the trademarked phrase "Smile" is owned by McDonalds.

Amazingly, advertising even exists on public television stations like Public Broadcasting System (PBS) and on commercial-free radio stations like National Public Radio (NPR). By design, these stations are not supposed to contain advertising. But they do. Advertising on these media is

called "sponsorship." Ads by sponsors are short and usually state that Corporation Whatever paid for the creation of
the program you are about to watch. Companies' motives in
giving away money, however, are more complex than simply
wanting to help the station. Corporations give away money
when it will help improve their public image, which is the
exact same reason they advertise. Giving money to PBS and
NPR allows sponsors to enjoy exclusive promotion during
the programs their donations fund. There's an added bonus,

too: sponsoring commercial-free programs occasionally allows corporations to influence the kinds of shows aired. In certain cases, sponsors have been allowed to censor, change, or cancel entire shows, or even to create new shows from scratch. Sponsorships sort of behave like paid programming and advertorials without labels. Pretty tricky, huh? Remember: every time you see a logo or hear a brand name, you are seeing or hearing an advertisement.

You may be surprised to hear that the Rule of Logos also applies to characters from TV, books, movies, and videogames. Whenever characters like Mickey Mouse, Lara Croft, Harry Potter, Wonder Woman, and SpongeBob SquarePants appear on merchandise, the owners of that character either paid or got paid for that placement. This sort of advertising is called "licensing." Advertisers like licensing because it's an ad double-whammy: you buy the shirt because you like the character, then you advertise that character to others by wearing the shirt. Even if people who see your shirt don't want to buy the same shirt, they may want to watch a movie or buy stickers that depict that character. This same principle allows "free" logo-covered toys to be given away with boxes of macaroni and cheese or bottles of fruit drink. Ads that mention both the name of the licensed character *and* a seemingly unrelated product are "cross-promoting." For example, a billboard that shows the cast of *Recess* consuming energy made possible by Sid R. Bass, an oil and gas refinery, acts as an advertisement for both the show and the energy company. A long time ago, cross promoting was when two different, non-competitive companies would help market each other because their products worked well together. Now you will often discover that the same company owns both the licensed character and stock in the product it's promoting. [Appendix F lists some holdings of big media companies.]

The Rule of Logos proves that advertisers and the media they influence are extremely sneaky about manipulating you into spending your money. But I think we can figure out a way to get them back.

Try This at Home

Walk around and shout "advertisement!" super loud every time you see a logo. Point to it. Do this at school, at home, in front of the TV; when you're reading magazines; and in the movies. Do it for a whole day, all day long. Do it with a friend if you feel dumb, or compete with a friend to see who can come up with more ad sightings in a day. If you want to be tricky, pronounce it with the accent on the second syllable like they do in England: *ad*-vurt-*iz-ment*. Maybe people will think you are from another country. If someone tells you to be quiet, try to figure out why. All you're doing is stating the truth. Maybe you're annoying your sister, who's trying to watch TV in peace after a hard day of kindergarten. (If so, you might want to stop making such a racket. Even kindergartners need a rest sometimes.) Maybe you're annoying your teacher, who's embarrassed that his classroom can't afford science experiments without Pizza Hut giving them to the school system. Tell him what you're doing. (Call it a media awareness study to get class credit for it.) Ask him where the school gets all the labeled and logoed promotional equipment. Be sure to tell your teacher it's not his fault society doesn't support his work in education and refuses to give his classroom the funding it needs.

2. IF YOU LOVE ME SO MUCH, WHY DON'T YOU ADOPT ME?

Now you're probably thinking, So what? I don't even *watch* commercials, and looking at a chart in math that compares nutritional values of brands of frozen peas doesn't affect me. A free stick of deodorant from my school does not make me a corporate slave. Reading a report in English on the costs of building prisons doesn't influence my spending habits, and the existence of sweatshops doesn't change my allowance. My clothes don't advertise anything. I hardly ever go to movies, I only listen to listener-sponsored community radio, and I live in a minuscule box in the bottom of the ocean where friendly whales bring letters from my family and sushi three times a day.

Actually, forget about the ocean thing. Maybe you think you're immune to advertising because you change the channel or mute the TV when commercials come on. Or maybe you simply don't like commercials as much as some people do. (Of course, people who wholeheartedly embrace advertising are worse off, since their whole world spins out of whack if they can't find the right hair product.) But no one is immune to advertising. *No one.* Advertising works by flattering you, confusing you, emulating you, and researching you. Then it pretends to be boring so you won't find out how much it influences you. And it all works.

In fact, people who think they're unaffected by advertising, are even more vulnerable to it than those who have never thought about it: since they don't ask themselves how they *might* be influenced by advertising, they don't notice when they *are*. In the film *The Ad and the Ego*, advertising researcher Jean Kilbourne said people often told her that advertising didn't influence them. She said she most often heard this from people wearing beer-logo baseball caps. However, she points out, advertising influenced them enough to wear a hat with an advertising message on it—a message that equates beer with near-naked, blonde ladies and athletic ability. In other words, the hat-wearers claim they're not influenced by advertising; they think their interests in beer-related clothing—and likely in the beer they are supporting—are natural. You probably know people who feel the same way about brands they like. Maybe you even feel naturally drawn to certain brands yourself. After all, being independent and rebellious (*rock and roll!!!!!*) is a great American tradition. Our country was founded on the pursuit of freedom, so admitting that we do what we are told to do by advertising is downright unpatriotic. Or worse, makes us feel like losers and followers. People support brands more fervently if they feel they are naturally drawn to them. But this is the biggest trick of advertising: getting people to believe that advertising doesn't affect them.

Advertising Works

We have to face facts. Advertising works on everyone. Companies spend enormous amounts of money on advertising. In-demand TV airtime alone (like during popular sitcoms, news specials, or the Super Bowl) can cost millions of dollars, not to mention the expense of producing a high-quality commercial. Advertising is expensive, and companies simply wouldn't pay so much money if they didn't get results. Of course what we see influences what we do, or businesses wouldn't spend money controlling what we see. Advertising works. We're just not sure how, or at least the audience isn't. And advertisers certainly won't tell.

I personally know advertising works, because it works on me. A few years ago, I wanted to buy a Saturn solely because the ads told me it was "a different kind of car." To this day, I honestly cannot tell you how a Saturn is different from any other kind of car—in fact, my research has shown that Saturns are *the exact same kind of car* as all other cars.

They have the same number of doors and drive the same speeds; they run on gasoline like other cars and are available in the same basic colors. Saturns fit the same number of people in them, cause a similar amount of pollution, and are even made by the same people as other cars. What made Saturn unique was a different kind of advertising. (Even knowing all this, I still have a soft spot for Saturns, although I have only been inside one once.)

Advertising Works on You

Advertising may work on everyone, but more messages are aimed at you than anyone else because companies love the youth demographic. "Demographic" is a marketing term used to describe the type of person a company targets to purchase its products. Demographics are based on common sets of characteristics or stereotypes. The stereotype of the youth demographic dictates that you are extremely brand loyal and have a lot of money to spend. In other words, you are one of the most sought-after ad targets right now because advertisers like you and your money.

Advertising Works by Flattering You

Advertising uses numerous tricks to win your affections on behalf of the advertised product, including flattery, confusion, co-optation (which means adopting cultural symbols), research, and your lack of knowledge about and interest in the corporate world. It's as if ads will do *anything* to get your attention. Advertisers like you so much, it may feel as if corporations are your only allies. Ads tell you about all the coolest games, clothes, and movies. Ads show you all sorts of pretty people you can act and dress like. Ads don't make you clean your room or take out the trash. Ads don't force you to take math tests. Ads don't ruin your favorite shirt or make out with your boyfriend. Ads seem really cool. But it's a trick. We'll look closely at how this trick works in the rest of this chapter. Pay close attention: there might be some good ideas you can steal for your own project.

To gain your favor, advertisers have created a couple of hip-sounding names for your age group: "kidz" and "tweens." This is a way of flattering you, telling you you're different from younger kids, but also a way of describing you as a desirable demographic. As we've seen, you are advertising's favorite demographic. When *I* use the word "kidz," I'm making a joke about this. I don't actually think of you as a demographic, but I think the realization that you *are considered* one by some people is important to keep in mind. You can fall for this flattery if you want to—it's probably true that you're super smart and beautiful and better in some ways than younger kids—but you don't have to do what ads tell you to do. Remember, ads aren't always truthful. Advertising needs to be a little dishonest, since we would never fall for advertising that told us what suckers we were. A TV commercial that proclaimed, "This product is no better than those produced by our competitors," or said "Big, dumb, stupid, jerks drink Crank Soda," would not sell many units, as funny as it would be to watch. Such ads do not positively distinguish products, which advertisers prefer to equate with happiness, health, intelligence, or exuberance. Some ads try so hard to equate their product with intelligence that they state their audience is too smart for advertising. (It's flattering to be called smart—so flattering you feel better about the product giving you this message.)

Advertising Works by Confusing You

Advertising can be confusing, however. It is easy to forget that the words and pictures for things are not the same as the things themselves. (Mixing up things with the words for them is called "reification.") So while it's dandy to learn about bouncability, spaghetti-sauce thickness, kidz, and flavor crystals, you have to keep in mind that those are just made-up words and phrases. Shampoo does not resolve a genetic lack of bouncability, the thickness of spaghetti sauce is entirely dependent on the amount of moisture in the recipe and not the "taste" or "freshness," "kidz" is a term used by the media to curry your favor, and scientists at the gum factory did not hit upon the solution to bad breath when they isolated the flavor crystal. These terms are made up by advertisers to sound sciencey. You can use them as much as you want to, but don't think for a second they're any more important or meaningful than anything you've ever made up yourself.

Advertising Works by Co-opting Your Culture

You've surely made up a word or phrase to describe something you and your friends talk about. Or maybe you have a nickname that comes from an inside joke other people wouldn't understand. Advertising does this too, although sometimes advertisers can't think of their own inside jokes, so they borrow them from you. This process is called co-optation. Co-optation has two related definitions: to co-opt is to take someone else's ideas, fashions, or manners as your own, and also to absorb entire groups into your own. Co-optation is when outsiders take over parts of another culture, often those that seem cutting edge, popular, cool, hip, or trendy. It can be a way of starting to remove another culture's unique identity. Clothing trends among the urban poor are co-opted by the fashion industry and new experiments in music show up quickly in videos by established performers and artists who didn't invent them. These are both extremely common examples of co-optation. And they work, even on the culture being co-opted.

For example, let's say that you and your friends are sitting around late at night during a sleepover drinking Wah-Tir!™ and making jokes about your baby sister's new Cutie Snugglefarb™ doll. One of the jokes is really funny, and your best friend laughs so hard he shoots Wah-Tir!™

straight out of his nose, all over Cutie Snugglefarb™, and all over you. When he stops laughing, he goes, "Oh, I just love Wah-Tir!™" in a funny voice. You and all your friends laugh and laugh and laugh until you practically pee in your pants, and from then on, for the next eight years, whenever someone says anything funny, one of you mimics your best friend saying "Oh, I just love Wah-Tir!™" in a funny voice. That's an inside joke. It's not a joke anyone would understand unless you explained it to them, and even then, they would probably have had to have been there to find it funny. If you saw one of your inside jokes in a commercial, it might convince you to purchase that product because you would feel like the ad "understands" you. Using the example above, if a TV commercial for Wah-Tir!™ ended with someone saying "Oh, I just love Wah-Tir!™" in a funny voice, you might start buying Wah-Tir!™ again because of it (even if it tastes like stale dust). If advertisers use your inside jokes—or your clothing style or mannerisms—they will seem like insiders to you. Co-optation gets you to overlook the fact that you're being told to buy something, so you skip right to identifying with the people in the commercial (who use those products exclusively, of course).

Often the media in general will emulate young adult behaviors to make you think you're among peers. As the education and media theorists Neil Postman and Charles Weingartner pointed out in *Teaching as a Subversive Activity*, most books for young adults use profane language. Why? Young adults don't swear any more or better than other people. In this book, for example, I'm trying to only use swear words when no other words will do, like I usually do in normal speech. I *could* swear like a motherfucker, but I hardly see the point. I don't want to trick you into thinking you're reading the work of a peer. Either you will respect what is written in this book and learn from it, or you will not. I urge you to be wary of anything that tries to speak to you in "your own" language. It's probably selling you something.

Advertising Works Because It Knows How You Work

Recently, companies figured out that youth and young adults influence about 45 cents out of every dollar spent in the United States. Between presents from grandparents, new clothes for school, snacks, and the government's domestic spending allowance, the opinions, hopes, and interests of youth are considered in almost half of all purchases in the U.S.! That's an enormous influence. And it's probably too large a money-making opportunity for most companies to pass up. Advertisers also trick you into liking them by placing kids for you to identify with in ads. Especially popular are ads featuring youth for products kids couldn't buy even if they had a humungous allowance, like vacations or cars. The companies that produce these ads have figured out two things about kids. One, you like to talk about what you see on television. Two, your family will do anything to get you to shut up about what you see on television even if it means buying the cereal, video game system, or car you want. Some ads even explain to kids the best ways to annoy their parents into buying certain things. Research (paid for by advertising firms) has even discovered that children's nagging was most effective when young people listed specific reasons for what they wanted. Thus, advertisers knew to put text (called "copy") into their ads to give you short, easy-to-remember reasons to purchase their products. An advertisement for the new Fasty-Drive™ Motor Vehicle, for example, might picture the vehicle with happy, cool-looking, young models in it, alongside copy describing how those youth convinced their parents to get a Fasty-Drive™ by refusing to take baths until their parents researched the increased safety measures available with the Fasty-Drive™. (One media-savvy girl told me she read somewhere it only took nine requests for a child to get what he or she wanted. I suspect she read it in an ad.) Advertisers have studied you and your whole family. I know it sounds creepy, but it's true.

Advertising Works by Pretending to Be Boring

Advertisers rely on your lack of interest in and limited knowledge about the corporate world. You don't know the secret networks and hidden history of companies—knowledge that keeps some older people from buying what they sell. You probably don't know, for example, that tobacco companies knew their products caused cancer before most smokers did and that automobile manufacturers take what they call "calculated risks" in allowing cheaper but more dangerous materials to go into vehicles, causing harm and death to drivers and passengers.

In fact, you're probably not even aware what companies produce which products! The connections can be weird and surprising. For example, veggie burgers aren't related to smoking. But the brand Boca Burgers is owned by Philip Morris (now calling itself the Altria Group), also the makers of Marlboro cigarettes. Moreover, the Altria Group owns Kraft Foods, Kool-Aid, and the company that owns Taco Bell, KFC, and Pizza Hut. Back when the Altria Group was called Philip Morris, they put up 900 million dollars to start a fake grass-roots organization named the Center for Consumer Freedom (CCF). (A grassroots organization is formed locally by community activists, while a fake grassroots organization—sometimes called an "Astroturf" organization—is formed by a corporation and pretends to be a grassroots organization.) The CCF calls itself a not-for-profit group dedicated to the protection of "consumer choices" (like smoking and eating fatty foods) against "food cops" (like health care workers concerned about obesity), "meddling bureaucrats" (like senators who push for restaurant anti-smoking legislation), and "violent radicals" (like activists who throw red paint on mink coats to protest the wearing of fur). Another tobacco giant, R. J. Reynolds, which makes one out of every four cigarettes smoked in the world (including Camels and American Spirit), owns a pharmaceutical drug company called Targacept that looks for positive medical uses of nicotine, the primary chemical found in cigarettes. R. J. Reynolds also owns Nabisco and Huffy. Mars, the maker of M&Ms, makes Uncle Ben's Rice Bowls and Whiskas, a snack for cats. Nike, primarily a seller of athletic shoes and clothes, recently attempted to open a hip, youth-friendly nightclub in Canada (named after one of its new shoe lines—that particular

**Altria Group
BAKE SALE**

Cookies! Burgers!
Smokes! Boxed mac'n'cheese!
THURSDAY, 11:00 – 1:00
Outside the Library

Come show your support for the increase of lung cancer and obesity! (free cruelty-heavy mink coats to first 100 customers)

[See "Graphic Design", p. 146; "Smoking and Drinking," p. 134; "Money," p. 139]

club didn't last long, though) and owns Hurley International, maker of teen clothing. Neopets, one of the most popular websites for kids ever created, is an extremely profitable business despite a lack of traditional ads or user fees to play on the site. Kids log on to visit their Neopet and earn Neopoints for certain activities, which can be used to feed, improve, or bathe their pets. The site turns a profit by using product placement (of Miramax, Kraft, and Disney goods, primarily) to hype advertisers' brands to kids. Neopets is owned by Dohring Marketing Research, a company designed to collect information about you to sell to advertisers. Neopets users can even earn Neopoints by filling out questionnaires and surveys about what they and their friends like to do and how they spend their money.

What does all this mean for you? Well, do you think it's a coincidence that your favorite musician appears on the cover of your favorite magazine, on the home page of your web browser, *and* has a new movie coming out, to be followed by a TV series as well as a line of comic books? It would be strange, except that all of these companies are often owned by one of the same parent companies. AOL, owned by Time

Warner, features "news" and "celebrity sightings" on its home page when you go to check your email. Sometimes this news relates to a movie coming out from New Line Cinema or showing on HBO, both owned by parent company Time Warner. Sometimes the news relates to whoever's on the cover of *Sports Illustrated* this week, or the *Time* Person of the Year. Both of these magazines are owned by Time Warner (so are *People* and *Entertainment Weekly*). In addition, Time Warner owns WB Pictures (the company that puts out the

Harry Potter movies—notice how Harry keeps showing up on your AOL page?), WB Television (makers of *Friends* and *The Bachelor*—castmembers from both shows regularly appear in *People* and *Entertainment Weekly*), WB Animation (which includes both Looney Tunes and Hanna-Barbera—cartoons made by these companies make jokes about movies by New Line Cinema or recording artists on Warner Brothers), and DC Comics (owner of superhero comics like Superman and *Mad Magazine*—ever wonder how *Mad* chooses movies to spoof?).

It starts to seem like the same few companies own everything. In a way, they do. Only a few companies control most media outlets, which means that a handful of people are behind most of the logos you come across in a day. The ten largest media companies in the world are Time Warner, General Electric, Viacom, the Walt Disney Company, Liberty Media Corporation, AT&T Corporation, News Corporation, Bertelsman, Vivendi Universal, and Sony. And nothing gets these companies more excited than kidz! [See Appendix F for a partial list of what these companies control.]

Advertisers Love Kidz!

Obviously, advertisers like you. It's nice to be liked, even for a dumb reason like being a target audience. I'll be honest, nobody else much cares what you do besides advertisers and the companies they work for. Of course, your parents, and the rest of your family love you (although they may not always know how to show it). Your friends love you, although they love other stuff too and don't have enough time for you. If you have an after-school club or are in a clique or gang, the other members of your clique, gang, or club love you. Maybe you have a dog or a cat or a snake or a pet cockroach and it loves you too.

Otherwise, you can't vote, which means politicians only care about you when you are a baby (and they can have pictures taken while kissing you) or when it can be proven in polls that people who *do* vote care about you. You can't legally work full time, so labor unions have no interest in you. You aren't voracious readers, so there are not as many great kids books as there are adult books, and publishers haven't added kids' sections to the *New Yorker*, the *Economist*, or the *Nation*. You can't own property, so you

31

can't join a neighborhood association or use property tax payments as a way to make your opinions count. You're supposed to be in school, so you can't join the PTA (even if you have children of your own). You don't watch the nightly news, so administrators get to do the TV interviews about the state of education or school lunch programs. You pretty much go to school, snack, do homework, watch TV, goof off with friends, play sports, eat meals, listen to music, play games, and make art. The scary part is that advertisers are in on all these activities. Because advertisers love kidz! This, in some ways, probably makes you feel wanted. Like everyone else, you want to be loved and you want to love things. Companies figure, why not love Shell Oil or Nike or Wendy's? If companies start getting friendly with you now, you are likely to retain fond memories of their products and support the companies that make them as you grow older. After all, parents are busier than they used to be. Many work outside the home, and more kids spend time alone because most other options (after-school programs, for example) have been shut down. Parents used to assume their children would care for them in their old age; companies now feel entitled to this treatment. In fact, if you glance around at your surroundings right now, I bet there are more logos than notes from your mom telling you she loves you. It's possible that advertisers love you more than your parents. (Some advertisers even ask your parents to prove their love by buying you things they can't afford.) What kidz offer advertisers is more valuable to them than love! That is why they use so many tricks to get in your good graces. Kidz offer advertisers minds free of knowledge of past corporate wrong-doings and current corporate holdings! Kidz offer a vast future earning potential! Kidz have a whole lifetime of spending ahead of them! So advertisers might not love *you*, they might just love your money.

Let's find out.

Try This at Home

Write to a company whose products you enjoy, whether it's Fox TV because of *The Simpsons* or Mars, Inc., because they make Twix. Explain how happy they make you. Then ask them to adopt you. Offer to live in the company president's office or house, or even in the factory if that sounds like more fun. Business people value well-written proposals, so be extremely descriptive and use the dictionary. Convince your family members to write you letters of recommendation. They surely won't want you to be adopted by a company, but they might think it's funny to see what happens. They can explain that you are a good child, not too messy, smart, small (compared to an adult), and easy to bathe (people often stretch the truth in letters of recommendation). Have them mention that you always loved the company's goods as much as, or more than, you have loved your own parents. If the company writes back and offers to adopt you, they probably do love you for more than your money and your potential for brand devotion. (You might at least be able to use this to argue for a better allowance at home.) But if the company sends you coupons, free gifts, and a nice letter with the company logo on it, they have just used your love for *them* as a way to do more advertising.

3. WHO IS THE BOSS OF YOU?

There was a time (like, in the Paleolithic era) when bathrooms didn't display ads and people couldn't conceive of shaving logos onto their heads, getting them tattooed onto their bodies, or airbrushing them onto police cars. School administrators used to refuse corporate sponsorships and forbid ads inside educational facilities. Now, most schools are too poor to turn down money. These days most everyone relies on money ("revenue") from advertising. When bands go on tour, they consider sponsorships. When people start magazines, they pay for printing with advertising. When schools need new computers, they accept them and all their logoed products from software companies. When your neighborhood kickball team needs new uniforms, they are paid for by a hardware store.

Think of all the jobs you could get that rely on advertising money: model, radio DJ, graphic designer, NASCAR driver, executive television producer, copywriter, and crazy scientist inventor-person. In general, we no longer question whether or not advertising is appropriate; we just accept that it is inevitable. The money it generates supports almost everything. People have even come to think of advertising as necessary. It's not, however. It's actually very damaging.

Advertising Is Everywhere, But That Doesn't Make It Important

Advertising is definitely ubiquitous, and it has become important to much of our culture. But *because* advertising is everywhere, and *because* we view it as necessary, we've begun to accept it as *natural*. Have you ever seen something without a logo—clothing, a concert, sports equipment—and thought it seemed cheap? We're so accustomed to logos and sponsorships that we sometimes don't think goods or events are possible without them. Would a concert be any fun if it weren't sponsored by Mountain Dew? Are athletic shoes even possible without Reebok, Adidas, or Nike? Did Mattel or Nintendo invent the concept of games? The ever-presence of logos implies that corporate ownership is crucial to every-day existence. But it's not. Neckties and bananas and video games and hand lotion aren't better because you recognize who makes or sponsors them. Games, music, and sports are all possible without corporations.

Yet we often hear that advertising keeps the costs of our magazines, concerts, newspapers, and TV shows low; we hear it subsidizes ticket prices. What you probably don't realize is that you pay those costs back whenever you buy advertised goods. *You* cover the costs of advertising when you purchase a satellite dish for your TV, get a bottle of water, or acquire big-name shoes. Sometimes advertising *does* make certain goods slightly less expensive. Newspapers, for example, are kept cheap by ad sales, and broadcast television is only possible (yet only worthwhile to corporations) because of its advertising potential. However, advertising also makes cheaply made goods cost more.

Advertising Costs Money, Space, and Time

Let's look at an example. Some of you may have heard about the terrible conditions in sweatshops, where workers are paid pennies to make hundreds of products per day. They work in unsafe conditions with poor air, few breaks, long hours, and no overtime pay. And you may have heard that name-brand shoes or clothes cost, say, $1.27 to make, compared to $130 to buy (or $89 on sale). This information is repeated often, but have you really thought about it? Even if each T-shirt or pair of shoes was shipped individually from a factory in Thailand directly to the retail store (Cost of box: $.50; Shipping charges: $10—although products actually travel by much slower, cheaper means), and if each product carried a $5 research-and-development cost *and* if the total price was doubled to cover the store's employee paychecks, the total bloated cost of each name-brand item would never be more than $33.54. So why do most clothes and shoes cost much more than that? The only cost we didn't factor in: advertising. Obviously, consumers cover the high cost of advertising.

Even those who admit that we do, eventually, pay for advertising still think of it as something to tolerate because it makes life easier. They see advertising as a necessary evil. Sure, it might add to the cost of some goods, but it lessens the cost of others, they argue. These people describe advertising by saying, "you scratch my back and I'll scratch yours," which is a phrase used to describe mutually beneficial relationships. If you scratch your friend's back, because it itches in a place she can't reach, or grab something from a high shelf for her, then she might scratch yours, or lend you a book. That's a fair exchange. You help your friend, and she helps you. Yet advertising isn't an equal relationship. It may help keep the costs of some things low—magazines, for example—but we also pay for advertising we might not want whenever we buy a pair of shoes, a CD, or a videogame.

Advertising is not mutually beneficial like back-scratching can be. When your friend scratches your back, you know it. She's doing it because you asked her to, and she would stop if you asked her to. But advertisers aren't going to stop showing ads, even if you ask. In fact, many deny that's what they're doing. Some of the kinds of advertisements we've mentioned in this book—sponsorships, product placements, or logos, for example—you doubtless didn't know were advertisements. Advertisers are making ads difficult to identify. Instead, you have to decipher sponsorships, product placements, promotions, advertorials, or paid programming. Can you imagine how annoyed you would be if you asked your friend to stop scratching your back, and instead she used a different technique and call it "super skin-relieftronic" or "not-front scritching"? Advertising is not mutually beneficial because it takes more than it gives. While advertising does provide information to consumers, clearly it is biased. And that biased information is about all advertising gives us. What it takes is our money, our space, and our time.

Advertising Makes Us Feel Bad

Perhaps even worse than costing money, space, and time, advertising damages our self-esteem. Here's how: the purpose of advertising is to get us to act in a way we normally would not. (Advertisers wouldn't bother spending money to persuade us to do something we were going to do anyway.) To get us to act, advertisers must make us feel as if something terrible were about to happen—to us—but that we could prevent it by buying their product. They want us:

- To buy Kohlfresch Toothpaste™ because we feel ugly and we think it will make our teeth whiter, which is supposed to be attractive;
- To wear Aktiv Shoes™ because we don't have much say in our lives right now and we believe we will feel more powerful if we own them;
- To eat Highpurr Breakfast Cereal with Marshmallows and Chocolate Syrup™ because we feel lonely and want to fit in, and it seems like everyone else eats it for breakfast;
- To drink Wah-tir!™ because we feel like dorks, and the people we find attractive say it tastes better than other beverages, and we feel cool doing what they do;

- To buy Stinkbadt Shampoo™ because sometimes we feel like *anything* will help and the "sheen" this shampoo provides will make us appear to have larger breasts, a more prominent scrotum, fewer zits, or will end our scourge of "bad hair days."

In other words, advertising gets us to act—that is, to buy advertised products—by making us *feel bad*. Advertising can control our emotions.

This is important: external controls over your moods are dangerous. It means you are not fully in charge of how you feel about yourself or anything else. Constantly being told that purchasing is the only way to be happy can make people feel dissatisfied and ineffective. Our advertising culture makes you feel as if you will never be able to keep up with every trend, and your stuff will not always be cool. (And advertising constantly reminds us how important cool is. Again, advertising controls our emotions. Like in a science fiction movie, a small number of people have found a way to manipulate a lot of other people.

Advertising Lies with Pictures If Not in Words

Since advertising relies on emotional response, it's difficult to sort out when it is being untruthful. Even a free textbook cover that carries a message of racial harmony illustrates that racial harmony is more likely with a certain kind of athletic shoe. That can't be true! Cigarettes, which cause cancer, are described as rebellious snacks, tickets to success, and refreshing gulps of freedom. But obviously they aren't! Advertisers are supposed to be honest in advertisements. They can't say, for example, that certain products will save your life if you use them before leaving the house, or that you will date people of the attractive sex 78 percent more frequently if you use a certain purchased good. But they can show things that aren't true.

While it may be illegal for an ad to say you will date 78 percent more often after using Smello™, it is legal to depict someone like yourself getting just that result. It is also permissible for a newscaster or a character in a sitcom to talk about their wonderful Smello™ experiences outside an official commercial. Advertisers may even insinuate, hint, or suggest that dating 78 percent more frequently is a direct result of Smello™ use.

The rules governing honesty in advertising apply only to what is said. Illustrating what advertisers can't state outright is an effective way to skirt those rules and still claim a result: a viewer could argue with the verbal claim that the product Smello™ gets users 78 percent more dates, but a viewer couldn't refute a video showing a gay man using Smello™ and then dating 78 percent more men. Like the boy in Minnesota proved, you can tell people not to try something at home, but if you also show them *how* to try it at home, that picture comes across as a conflicting message. The media may say, "Don't try this at home," before an MTV *Jackass* episode that shows people how to light themselves on fire, but which message is stronger, the verbal message that you shouldn't try this at home, or the visual message that shows you how cool it would be to try?

The problem, in some ways, is the very concept of truth in advertising. If an ad makes a false verbal claim, we can argue against it. But if an ad makes no verbal claim, and instead shows us what *might* happen through use of a product, a viewer cannot refute that claim. Ads use metaphors—often visual—to make statements about products. With visual metaphors, it is difficult to say what is true and what is false. It is said there is no universal concept of truth. All definitions of truth are created to achieve certain purposes. Truth in science class is different from truth in art, and may change depending on the time and location you study. Unfortunately, it is difficult to enforce the concept of truth in advertising because not everyone agrees on the definition of truth *or* the definition of advertising.

The visual metaphors used by advertising to give viewers an emotional sense of truth. People can learn quickly by using metaphors, but metaphors can be dangerous if you forget about them. If you are a gay man and have seen the ads for Smello™, you may expect to date more often after purchasing Smello™. Of course, when you think about it, you know this product does not control your social life, but you still have an image in the back of your mind that guides your thinking. Even if you used Smello™ and got exactly 0 percent more dates because of it, you might still think of it as a successful product and continue buying it because of

Retail Therapy

Listed below are several leading brands, their slogans, and the social problems young adults face today. Many products solve a number of problems simultaneously, although a double application is not always necessary to achieve this result.

PRODUCT	SLOGAN	YOUNG ADULT'S SOCIAL PROBLEM
Aktiv Shoes™	"For Your Active Life"	Obesity, Unpopularity, Ugliness, Stupidity*, Laziness
Crank Soda™	"Whoa!"	Sleepiness, Depression, Malnutrition
Cutie Snugglefarb™	"Isn't She the Cutest?!?"	Disinterest in procreation, Disinterest in fashion, Disinterest in objectifying women and girls
Fasty-Drive™ Motor Vehicles	"When You Want to Feel Safe, Just Look For the Fasty-Drive™ Logo"	Pervasive fear (of death by vehicular collision, of loss of natural resources, of foreign cars and related industries, of foreigners, of not fitting in, of homosexuality, of loneliness, of nature)
Friends of Fasty-Drive™	"A Grassroots Consumer Awareness Organization"	Disinterest in purchasing Fasty-Drive™ Motor Vehicles
Half-Hour of Fun	[Television program; no slogan]	Poor casual conversation skills, Inability to relate to others, No social life outside of work or school

Highpurr Breakfast Cereal with Marshmallowsand Chocolate Syrup™	"Really Gets You Going!"	Malnutrition, Lack of energy
Kohlfresch Toothpaste™	"By MegaMedTech, Inc. Thanks, MegaMedTech, Inc.!"	Bad breath*
LaserSaw™	"Never Suffer From Hangnails Again! Another useful product from MegaMedTech, Inc."	Hangnail pain, Unpopularity resulting from bleeding hangnails, Depression resulting from hangnail pain, High hangnail-sufferers suicide rate
Lindsay K. Streisand-Fitzhugh Gubernatorial Campaign	"A Vote for Streisand-Fitzhugh for State Governor is a Vote for America"	Lack of patriotic pride, Not knowing who to vote for
Pretty McQueen™	"So Adorable!"	Disinterest in procreation, Disinterest in fashion, Disinterest in objectifying women and girls, Loss of interest in Cutie Snugglefarb™ due to overmarketing
Smello™	"Date More"	Loneliness, Unpopularity, Persistent foul smell*
Stinkbadt Shampoo ™	"Fuck. That Smells Good."	Dirty hair*
The Show with That Guy	[Television program; no slogan]	Boredom*
Wah-tir!™	"Over 17 % Natural Ingredients"	Dehydration, Malnutrition

*actual scientific results in alleviating these problems were inconclusive the image in your mind. Or, if you were me, you might realize that Saturns are exactly the same as any other car, but you might still like them for no obvious reason.

All Media Act Like Advertising

All forms of advertising are subsets of media. Commercials are a part of TV and radio, billboards are a part of public space and print media, and pop-up ads and spam are a part of the Internet. These forms of advertising—everything covered by the Rule of Logos—is direct advertising. Direct advertising is when a company wants you to support a specific product, good, or service. Yet the media are also businesses that want your continued support. The media have agendas of their own, and they use many of the same tricks as advertisers to get you to support these agendas. Sometimes these agendas swing toward corporate support, and sometimes they are more governmental.

Propaganda, or information put out by an organization or the government in order to promote an idea, policy, or cause, is an important concept to keep in mind when talking about the media. Although the term has a negative connotation, it is an accurate word to describe the underlying policies that guide corporate and governmental advertising, media, and public relations. The metaphors used in corporate and governmental propaganda are especially powerful because they allow us to forget, for example, that our dinner was manufactured by a tobacco firm or that our favorite TV channel is operated by people that profit from war. Or we might forget that the cute character on our new backpack makes money for a company that believes all video rentals for young adults should be free of swear words, nakedness, and homosexual themes. What dinner we eat, what TV channel we watch, and who edits the videos we rent all affect what we see; and what we see controls our behavior and could change what we believe.

The media did not begin emulating advertising so directly overnight. It was a gradual process. When companies first realized how frustrating and annoying people found ads, they made advertising more subtle so they wouldn't lose viewers. Commercials started making fun of advertising and product placement became the brunt of jokes, even though it didn't stop. Imagine a movie about a punk-rock band, for example,

where all the band members joke that they wouldn't ever sell
out to a big corporation—except the makers of Kohlfresch
Toothpaste™. Maybe every time they showed or talked about
Kohlfresch Toothpaste™ in the movie, all the band members
would pause and look at a tube of the toothpaste lovingly, and
some meaningful, classical music would play in the back-
ground. This sort of scenario happened in several movies in
the last few years. Also popular were ads that stated clearly,
"We're advertising something, so we're going to lie to you

now." Ads started looking more and more like games or documentary videos or science experiments or fashion and less and less like ads. (Even if you didn't yell "advertisement!" every time you saw a logo on something, you'd perhaps still realize advertising is everywhere, and it doesn't always look like an ad).

Now, however, everything we consume for entertainment is infected with the spirit of advertising. Through product placements, advertorials, sponsorships, and other similar methods of direct advertising, the division between ad and not-ad in the media has eroded completely.

Let's look at TV as an example. Think about when your favorite TV show has a character appear from another show you don't watch: it's called a "crossover." That guy from *The Show with That Guy*, for example, may make a guest appearance on the sitcom *Half-Hour of Fun*. For that half-hour, *Half-Hour of Fun* introduces you to that guy and gives you a bit of an idea of what his show is about. It makes you consider watching the show and you may even watch it immediately, since it is most likely programmed directly after *Half-Hour of Fun*. Although it's just a regular show, it's also an advertisement for *The Show with That Guy*, since the point is to get you to watch that show. Similar crossovers occur on news or chat programs: Often talk-show guests have their own TV show on the same network, or perhaps the news is about an event relating to the production or crew of a TV show on that network. Sometimes talk-show guests appear to chat about their new movie, put out by the same parent company of that network. Occasionally, guests discuss a new product manufactured by, you guessed it, the same company. The point of all these crossovers is to get you to consume the parent company's other media programs or products. Often, when you watch a news or chat program, you've just seen more propaganda.

All Media Have an Agenda

Some people think that even when TV, radio, magazines, the Internet, or newspapers don't show specific products, they *still* contribute to an atmosphere of consumerism. That is, even when you watch TV or movies and don't see any logos, you are still being urged to purchase. A story about cancer-causing breast implants or a report of the Dow Jones

Industrial Average does not tell you to purchase specific things. Such news stories do, however, avoid aspects of stories that *don't* relate to spending money. Stories about breast implants causing cancer, for example, do not focus on what in society causes women to *want* breast implants, they focus instead on the procedure to remove breast implants, or on the high cost of cosmetic surgery. (Stories about the effects of breast implants may also make cosmetic surgery seem normal.) Similarly, reports on the economy mention the Dow Jones Industrial Average, a number that tracks the stock market, but don't list membership numbers in labor unions, even though both are potential measurements to describe the health of the labor force and economy.

Even during regular programming (meaning, not during commercials or ads), the media focus on the amount of money people spend. Shopping is a popular sitcom activity, and many a family drama has been inspired by the loveable father character's purchase of an expensive new gadget he doesn't want his wife to know about. Kids on shows are constantly saving money to purchase objects or attend events; crime and mystery programs often hinge on whether or not the perpetrator stole money. On the Internet, character-based interaction sites like Gaia and Neopets allow you to manipulate your character based on the amount of money you have accrued. Morning radio DJs often give away cash or prizes to lure you into listening, or into identifying a specific band's catchy new single, which has just gone on sale at stores near you. Although you may not see a logo or hear a brand name, you are constantly reminded of the availability of products to consume. This isn't a total shock; we live in a consumer culture. But it is surprisingly difficult to find stories in the media that have nothing to do with consumption. The media portray, almost exclusively, what people buy and in what quantities. For example, the news used to report ticket sales and crazy fan antics when discussing big movie openings. Now, weekend grosses are reported. By focusing on consumerism, the media have become little more than propaganda tools for products, companies, politicians, government programs, and government actions.

Even Your Friends Help Promote
the Agenda Set by Advertising

With your peers, too, it's hard to tell where regular talk stops and advertising begins. In addition to chat among classmates about favorite commercials, new clothes, and videogames, some youth are paid big money to go out and hype particular brand names. This is called guerilla marketing. Sometimes, guerilla marketing takes the form of club kids, who are super-cool looking youngsters paid to dance at fancy clubs in big cities. Other times, reps for big music companies pay hip college students to hand out free CDs to their friends. Those bands then become popular on college radio, an influential and lucrative music market, and among college students, who are always looking to purchase the next big thing. PR firms, market analysts, and advertisers have all paid youth to talk about what's already cool in their neighborhoods and to make new things cool among their friends. Cigarette companies hire pretty scenester girls or tough-lookin' punkers to hand out free packs of smokes in bars so their brand becomes associated with attractive girls or coolness. It's like peer pressure, but it's not just for kids anymore.

Even though advertising seems harmless, it costs you money, space, time, and emotional health. It lies to you and manipulates you, and forces you to view the world the way coporations and the government want you to. That's the bad news. The good news is that we can change all that.

Try This at Home

Spend a day without consuming a single advertising message. Don't watch TV or movies, don't read magazines with ads (some, like zines your friends may make or *Ms.*, don't run ads), don't listen to the radio, don't go to events, don't talk to friends who mention brand names, don't spend time with anyone wearing a logo on their clothes, don't look at any food packaging or go inside fast-food restaurants. Don't sing jingles or hum them quietly to yourself. Don't buy candy, don't play videogames that use product placement, and don't allow anyone to mention any mass-produced objects to you all day long.

Actually, you know what? Don't try this after all. It would be boring. You would have to paint every single thing in your room black and stay inside all day, unless you live next to a National Forest (and even those have occasional sponsorships on signage and inside gift shops and snack stands.) Trying to spend a day without advertising would be like a fish trying to spend a day without water, and I wouldn't ask a fish to do that.

Try This Instead

Call the 800-number on the back of your favorite food package and tell them your age and how popular you are in school. (Feel free to inflate these numbers. Advertisers do.) Explain that as a respected member of a sought-after demographic with vast peer influence, you have assisted the growth of their company in innumerable ways without compensation. Offer your exclusive services as a guerilla marketer. Request to be paid for each mention of their brand to your friends. Explain that although you are loyal to their brand, you would become even more loyal to a competing brand if that competitor were to give you more money. The company will surely turn down your generous proposal, but if they don't, and they offer you *any* amount of money, ask if they will double it. See if they'll spend their entire advertising budget for the year on you. To sweeten the deal, offer to make all their commercials for them if they give you a fully-equipped studio. Tell them you're really clued in to the lucrative youth demographic. Maybe they'll go for it, and you'll have an even better reason to like that company: they pay you to. (Remember to be honest about this when you make those commercials.) If they finally turn you down, however, and you ever mention their brand again, keep in mind that the company wasn't willing to give you money to tell people about it.

4. IT'S SORT OF A FREE COUNTRY

The media, of course, don't really control the universe, but they *have* so saturated society that politics only exist, for many people, in the way they are portrayed in the media. Yet if we look closely at how this works, we might be able to figure out what politics really are, and what you can do to change the world.

Media theorist Neil Postman's book *Amusing Ourselves to Death* gives an example of how TV affects politics: it is mandatory that all U.S. presidential candidates be reasonably good looking and have a pleasant, yet commanding, speaking voice. (Can you imagine a viable candidate that was obese, or one whose nose whistled while speaking? Have you ever seen a candidate with a disfigurement, an obvious flaw, a punk-rock hairstyle, or a permanent, gaping wound?) An easy-on-the-eyes image is mandatory because candidates *must appear on television*. If a candidate isn't televisually appealing, the candidate won't be elected. Basically, the presidency of the United States of America is decided based on his, or soon her, entertainment value.

In the same way, the only things ever considered "news" are noteworthy events with interesting televisual elements to them. While poverty, homelessness, drug abuse, and child neglect are constant concerns, deserving of regular attention and discussion, they are not shown on television as often as they occur in our culture (all day long, every single day). These issues are discussed only when connected to an unusual, shocking, violent crime. This is because these conditions do not suddenly change, so they are not considered newsworthy. And since the most-afflicted participants are not televisually appealing, the media usually overlook them. Unfortunately, this means poverty, homelessness, drug abuse, and child neglect are ignored most of the time by both the media and society. This is how the media control what we think of as enraging, important, and political.

The Media Are Influenced by PR

This is not a coincidence. The media's version of politics is controlled primarily by an industry called public relations (PR for short). PR firms are secret, behind-the-scenes groups that evaluate and influence public opinion. They are hired to create positive regard for big businesses and government agencies; they act like advertisers but don't call what they do advertising. PR does not receive as much attention as advertising because the government doesn't like to admit it needs to advertise to its own people. Nor do corporations wish to be seen blatantly manipulating the media. Government and big business don't want the public to know how much propaganda goes into the media. Both the government and big businesses want the media to appear authentic and objective. PR is often secretive and deceitful.

The public gets angry when they discover that government and corporations actively try to manipulate—as opposed to respond to—public opinion. People don't like to be manipulated, so PR firms work secretively. They rarely write plans down in case papers are leaked to newspapers; employees use fake names and invent false committees; and sometimes the firms deny they are in the business of public relations at all! How sneaky is that?

PR Affects What You Think About and How You Think About It

PR firms have to act secretively, because if people knew how often and how easily they were manipulated, they would no longer trust the governmental agencies and businesses that used those tactics. Sheldon Rampton and John Stauber's book, *Trust Us, We're Experts*, provides a great example of how PR works. In the early 1990s, a group in Australia called MOP (Mothers Opposing Pollution) started complaining about plastic milk cartons. The group, which claimed to be the largest women's organization in the country, was headed by a woman called "Mrs. Alana Maloney." The group objected to plastic containers due to the difficulty of recycling them, the creation of cancer-causing agents in milk stored in plastic, and the loss of vitamins that occurs when milk is exposed to light. Mothers everywhere were urged to stop purchasing milk in plastic containers. However, the only member of MOP to appear in public was "Mrs. Maloney," and reporters became suspicious. First, they discovered that all the "offices" MOP claimed to have throughout Australia were post-office boxes. Then, they discovered that "Mrs. Maloney" was the fake name of Janet Rundle, head of a PR firm called J. R. and Associates. Rundle's firm was working for another PR firm that was working for a manufacturer of *paper* milk cartons.

See how this works? It's super tricky. It's sort of like someone paying your brother to cry every time you put on a shirt with Cutie Snugglefarb™ so you would learn to like rival Pretty McQueen™ better. Or like paying your best friend to always talk about a certain problem (say, the high cost of taxes) and their ideas for a solution to it (say, elect

Lindsay K. Streisand-Fitzhugh governor). Actually, this last idea is not far-fetched at all. PR firms, like advertisers, already use peers to directly influence your decisions.

As these examples show, public relations practices are not limited to manipulating the public's view of brand-name products. PR firms also shape public opinion on drastic matters, like safety, violence, disease, and war.

Historians say that PR got its start in the late 1920s when Edward Bernays was hired by the American Tobacco Company to convince more women to smoke cigarettes. Instead of using print ads, such as the Lucky Strikes campaign of that time period that urged women to smoke instead of eat sweets, Bernays convinced ten women to march and smoke in the Easter parade in New York. He called their cigarette smoking a protest against women's inequality, and nicknamed the event the "torches of freedom" parade (the cigarettes were the torches of freedom). Because smoking was considered socially unacceptable for women, the idea of women smoking in public was, at the time, scandalous. Newspapers all over the country ran the story with pictures on the front page. Soon, smoking became enormously popular among women. Eighty years later, the surgeon general announced that smoking caused the premature death of at least one woman every three and a half minutes.

Another example occurred in the 1980s, when it was discovered that free samples of Nestlé's infant formula, given away in third world countries, were killing babies. Instead of ceasing distribution of the formula, Nestlé brought in a PR firm to fight boycotts of its products. The main problem with the infant formula was that it had to be mixed with water—and clean drinking water is impossible to find in many third world countries. Worse, mothers were persuaded to use the free samples when Nestlé claimed the formula was healthier for babies, and that if mothers loved their children they would use it. Often, use of the first free sample disrupted the mother's production of breast milk, and she was forced to continue using the Nestlé formula, which now had to be purchased. Some reports estimated the resulting infant deaths at around 1.5 million per year. During the 1980s, however, fast-acting PR let people in the

U.S. ignore Nestlé's baby-killing for a while so they could concentrate on its chocolate bars.

In the 1990s, the Water Pollution and Control Federation (a fancy-sounding name for an organization that manages PR for, and lobbies on behalf of, the sewage industry) decided to change the name of "sludge" to "biosolids." (Another fancy sounding name for a bacteria- and virus-filled combination of organic material, toxic metals, synthetic chemicals, and settled solids from wastewater treatment plants. In other words, dangerous but cleaned-up poo.) In 1992, the Environmental Protection Agency (EPA) modified the technical standards regulating the use of this material as fertilizer on farmland. Changing the name, according to Rampton and Stauber's *Toxic Sludge is Good for You*, turned the same substance—considered highly dangerous when it was called sludge—into something considered safe to dump on food crops. Since then, farmers that use biosolids as fertilizer, as well as their neighbors, have noted significant health problems in farm animals and family members, including persistent coughs, unusual viruses, and cancers. (As this book went to press, a new proposal was being considered to again change the name of "biosolids" to "compost.")

Most recently, a massive PR campaign was put in place prior to the 2003 Iraq War. This war, the first in history to be protested by millions before it even began, was opened to reporters under a program called "embedding," an idea developed by Assistant Defense Secretary Victoria Clarke. Clarke previously worked for the PR firm Hill and Knowlton, which was involved in an incident that occurred a couple of months prior to the first Gulf War in 1991. At that time, U.S. news agencies heard a story that Iraqi soldiers had entered hospitals in Kuwait, ripped premature babies from incubators, and dropped them on the floor to die. A fifteen-year-old Kuwaiti girl named Nayirah claimed to have been a hospital volunteer and witness to the massacre. She spoke to the Congressional Human Rights Caucus, which agreed to keep her identity a secret to shield her from danger. Later, Nayirah's last name was discovered, and she turned out to be the daughter of the Kuwaiti ambassador to the United States. She had never seen anything like the hospital scene she had described for the caucus. It was also discovered that the entire caucus—and Nayirah's appearance there—had been set up by Hill and Knowlton, who had been paid by the Kuwaiti royal family. It was all a plot to raise U.S. support for the Gulf War, according to Stuart Ewen's *PR! A Social History of Spin*.

Victoria Clarke's "embedding" brainstorm was only one of many PR tactics created to manufacture support for the 2003 Iraq War. By reporting alongside soldiers, journalists lost their sense of objectivity and adopted, according to media critics, an inappropriate sense of loyalty to U.S. soldiers. More than one reporter tripped up and referred to the U.S. military's actions as "our actions," or the U.S. troops as "our side." Some even used phrases like "we bombed . . . " or "we attacked . . ." These phrases call into question the journalists' abilities to report facts accurately, since they identify so strongly with one side in the battle. Even outside the U.S., many fingers point toward PR as a cause of this war. Alistair Campbell, British Prime Minister Tony Blair's advisor and the so-called Minister of Spin, was forced to resign after reports that he had "embellished" information (meaning, made it up) about Saddam Hussein's weaponry. As this book goes to press, questions continue to circulate about George Bush's deception in demanding war against Iraq. There's no telling to what degree PR will be held responsible.

PR, Advertising, and the Media Dictate What People Think of as Political

Of course, PR tactics can't work without the active participation of the media and its traditional advertising techniques. One extremely common example of the powerful partnership among advertising, the media, and PR is the video news release (VNR for short). A VNR is created by PR firms, on behalf of governmental and corporate clients, to promote an idea, a company, or a product. VNRs are filmed exactly like conventional news reports, but without the supposed objectivity independent reporters might provide. Completed VNRs are sent to news stations and aired on the evening news like regular reports. No one explains that they were made to promote an idea, a company, or a product; no one explains that they weren't created by the station and its reporters. VNRs are simply slipped into news broadcasts like regular reports. One PR person estimated that 80 percent of all evening news broadcasts consist of VNRs.

NewsProNet, one company that supplies VNRs to news stations, was taken to task in 2003 for shoddy journalism and ambiguous ethics when it was discovered that a Bay Area NBC TV station used its services. NBC 11 ran a sensationalistic headline and a story filled with inaccuracies that was traced back to NewsProNet's services (detailed at www.newspronet.com). The description for one of NewsProNet's services reveals the point of VNRs: marketing. "Fresh content that sets you apart from your competition, smart content that appeals to key demographic segments of your audience, and credible content your staff will be proud to stand in front of," NewsProNet's web site proclaims. Nowhere does the company claim to provide important, relevant, objective news stories to help people make decisions about their daily lives.

Yet NewsProNet is still used, and NewsProNet and such "content" companies continue to infuse our media with biases, falsities, and boring, mistake-ridden stories. Can you imagine how a history textbook would read if 80 percent of it were written by someone who didn't believe in the letter "k," *really* liked cheese, or thought that only reptiles were worth writing about? It would alter your view of what happened in history. Our views of the present are being altered in the same way by PR tactics and advertising techniques.

To give you a concrete example of how a VNR may influence you, imagine that the fake company MegaMedTech Inc., the makers of the LaserSaw™, approved a VNR created by a PR firm that describes an exciting new breakthrough in the treatment of hangnails. The LaserSaw™, a machine that cures you of hangnails by cutting off your hand with a painful, humming, whirring laser, is featured in the VNR as a reliable treatment for troublesome hangnails. The VNR shows doctors talking about how *people hate hangnails.* Basically, it looks like regular news. Except the next time you get a hangnail, you think immediately about that great new technology, the LaserSaw™, and you sign up to get your hand cut off. (Did you notice? Right in the middle of the broadcast is a logo. And you know what that means.)

You're going to have to use your imagination to figure out what advertising and PR could convince people to do. They have already convinced some people that Nestlé is a nice company, that NBC has totally objective news reports, and that the color of Christina Aguilera's hair is important. These are dumb but destructive lies spread by TV. News stories like these keep you from thinking about real political issues.

The World Before Aktiv Shoes

An Historical Treatise

Over ten years ago, when dinosaurs roamed the earth, there was a terrible tragedy of no one having any decent footwear. Scientists often speculate that this tragedy, indeed, is the exact reason for the extinction of dinosaurs: because dinosaurs became extinct when meteors came down and hit them all on the head, a fast running shoe could easily have saved the species. And this would be great, because now we could all have pet dinosaurs to ride to school!

[one]   **The World Before Aktiv Shoes!**

But that is not the point. This is not a zine called HOW TO GET TO SCHOOL, this is a zine called THE WORLD BEFORE AKTIV SHOES, and it is a wonderful little historical treatise about the great tragedy no one likes to think about.

The World Before Aktiv Shoes!   [two]

Anyway, in this time I was talking about, before the shoes and everything, some other stuff happened and then cities formed and then god invented the Olympics as a sporting arena through which various countries could spite each other without actually launching a full-scale military attack. Because of the Olympics, scientists developed a strategy for discovering exactly who the world's best basketball player was, and he didn't have enough to do when he was off the court, so Aktiv Shoes were invented so he could talk about them on TV for a hobby.

[three]   **The World Before Aktiv Shoes!**

Suddenly, the clouds parted. It only rained on farmland and all the dogs in the world who ever ran away
came back to their owners and poverty was abolished
and everyone's hair developed instant bouncability.

The World Before Aktiv Shoes!   [four]

Aktiv Shoes made people happy. Not just OK about their footwear, but truly satisfied on a spiritual level. Not only that, but it gave them the ability to escape tiger attacks and enter runs for MS. It wasn't just the shoes, though: it was the clothes, the feeling of belonging, the logo, the way of life. Aktiv Shoes make you feel like you are wearing active shoes. And this is no mere coincidence.

[five]   **The World Before Aktiv Shoes!**

The moral of the story is that everything before Aktiv Shoes sucked ass. All of history was so lame, it didn't even need to have happened! Except for Aktiv Shoes. They do not suck ass. They are wonderful!!!!!

THE END

p.s. don't drink and drive!

You Don't Need the Media to Define Politics for You

Politics, after all, is *not* just a subject in school, or something practiced by older, white men on C-SPAN. In fact, I think politics is the science of government, the activities of a political party, and all political opinions. If you don't believe me, look "politics" up in the dictionary. Remember: books are part of the media. I could be wrong or lying to you. I'm not, but question everything in this book anyway. It's too easy to believe something because it's written down and it's equally easy to write down untruths (like the premature babies story from Kuwait) or show things on TV that never happened (like Smello™ getting you 78 percent more dates).

Politics is actually how people, either alone or in groups, feel about their surroundings and act on their feelings. Also, it's the study of how people have felt about their surroundings and acted on their feelings in the past, which is when politics gets called a science, like history. If, for example, you hated the school lunch menu and got the administration to add more vegetarian options, that would be a political act. So, politics is when you want to change something about the world.

"Politics" appears in the dictionary fairly near where the word "poetics" would appear, if it were in my dictionary. Since my dictionary doesn't list the word "poetics," and yours might not either, let's combine the definitions of poem, poet, poetic, and poetry, to figure out what poetics is: of or pertaining to creative expression; a disregard for standard forms of writing in favor of imaginative communication; a deviation from form; and a description of the way the world could or should be. In other words, poetics is when you think about the world differently than how it appears.

Clearly, politics and poetics are sort of opposite things. When you think politically, you try to change the world. When you think poetically, you try to imagine how the world could be different. But if you combine the two, you decide the world should be different and set about telling people how or why. Sometimes this is called art and sometimes it's called activism. People who work politically *and* poetically all the time just call it work. We'll call it artistic activism and discuss more ideas for it in the next section of this book.

You Are Already Political

As we've already figured out from examining the media, just because something isn't on the news or in the dictionary or on your web browser or in your favorite magazine, doesn't mean it's not important. We were able to define "poetics" even though it isn't in some dictionaries. Keep in mind that sometimes the information you need is hidden behind the information available. Like how advertisements state a sandwich is 58 percent fat-free, when actually the sandwich is 42 percent fat. Sometimes information, like the definition of poetics, is hidden because no one thinks it's important. At other times, information is hidden because it's considered dangerous. It's not exactly dangerous that your sandwich is 42 percent fat (unless you have such a terrible heart condition that the next sandwich will kill you), but a sandwich advertised as 42 percent fat almost certainly won't sell, and that's dangerous to the company that makes those sandwiches. So, the fact that a sandwich is 42 percent fat is kept hidden because it is dangerous information. The fact that politics is how you think about your surroundings and act on those feelings might also be dangerous.

If we can agree that politics is when you decide or desire to change something about the world, why don't more people consider themselves political? Why don't you think of politics as something you already do? Perhaps the idea of you practicing politics at home is dangerous to career politicians because they don't want any competition, and they certainly don't want people accomplishing things at home that they get paid to do (or not do) in the government. It makes career politicians seem useless. Perhaps it's easier for our government if you stay unpolitical. Keeping politics exclusively in the government means politicians don't have to ask very many people what to do when they make decisions. Perhaps corporations would prefer you stay unpolitical because they don't need anyone meddling in their plans. Therefore, to the government and big business, it may be dangerous for you to think of yourself as political, just as it is dangerous to the sandwich company that you see their product as 42 percent fat.

We know that if the government and big business felt like it, they could make a lot of people feel ineffective and unpolitical through their most powerful tool, the media. This may be why so many kids think politics is something only politicians can do. But now you know that being political means what you think about and how you act. You are already political.

Since You Are an Important Marketing Demographic, You Are Also an Important Political Demographic

You can't help but be political. You already think that how things *are* is only one of many options for how things *could be*.

Surely you think the state of your world *should* be better. Maybe you even have ideas for *how* it could be better. If not, that's ok, because it's always enough to raise issues and ask questions. You also know now that the media love kidz! This is important because it proves *you* have power over the media.

Susan J. Douglas explains in her book *Where the Girls Are* that girls growing up watching TV in her generation, "became one of the most important things any group can become in America: A market. . . . Once you become a market—especially a really big market—you can change history" (p. 24). Right now, you kidz are in a unique position to change the world!

And changing the world is easy. Before you ever heard of this book, you had probably already thought of creative ways to start to do it. Writing a poem, for example, or writing a letter to your congressperson. Not eating certain kinds of food or going to certain stores. Reducing, reusing, and recycling. Avoiding specific magazines or not watching certain kinds of TV shows. There are a zillion other ways. I'll try to list some in the next chapter and give you detailed instructions in the Ways and Means section of this book, but I'm sure you'll be able to think of many more on your own.

Changing the world only takes three simple steps. It's so easy! First, you have to communicate your idea. Second, you have to get your community to help you implement your idea. Third, you have to broadcast your idea to the wider public and get them to help you implement it, too. All you have to do is figure out what to change about the world first.

Try This at Home

Make a list of ten ways the world can be improved. Write it down and look it over. Decide if any of these things are worth spending a few hours working on. (If none are, start over.) Research your favorite ideas a little on the Internet or by talking to family, teachers, or during crank calls to China. See if there are any groups you want to join that already work on similar ideas. If there are, and you like joining groups, call them up and tell them you want to help. If there aren't any groups to join, or you don't like groups, check out if there's anything you can do by yourself or with a friend, or start your own group. The last time I made my list, it looked like this:

1. Mandatory cat ownership for all U.S. citizens (except the allergic)
2. Free ice cream!
3. Public transportation that runs on human waste
4. Cooperative military and psychology training programs that give all psych students patients and all military personnel long-term mental health programs
5. Study abroad programs for middle-schoolers
6. Cheaper housing for artists and writers
7. Zero-waste programs for all civic buildings: in-house plants that recycle all paper and plastic used by employees and visitors on the premises
8. More stringent laws controlling corporate use of space and sponsorships
9. More information for kids about how they can influence the media and politics
10. Roving gardens in the back of every pick-up truck

When I looked my list over, I decided to write a book based on number nine. That's what you're reading now.

5. GET EVERYONE ELSE TO FOLLOW THE LEADER

When I said there are only *three* steps to you influencing the way the world works, I lied. Bwah-ha-ha-ha! What did you expect? A book is a part of the media! Really there are four steps. The first is that you must learn to say "Bwah-ha-ha-ha!" like an evil scientist. Since this is a book, I cannot demonstrate this skill. Find an evil scientist to help you master it. Following this, you must convince your friends and family that your idea is a good one. Then, alert the greater community, meaning your neighbors and local and federal governments, of the possibility in your idea. Finally, you must broadcast your message to the rest of the world. Once you have mastered the laugh *and* told all these people your great idea, changing the world will be easy, although it may take a while. Pack a lunch and stick ten bucks in your sock in case you have to call a cab.

Convince Your Friends and Family

Your first step is the easiest one. You already influence friends and family all the time; you may not even be aware of it. Have you ever noticed friends copying you, picking up little phrases you made up, drawing like you, or wearing a style of clothes similar to yours? That is all a kind of influence, although you might call it copying or emulation. (Bwah-ha-ha-ha!)

It's the same kind of influence that the media have over people. An annoyingly large number of popular phrases come from TV. (Have you ever said "D'oh!" "Just do it," or "one *meeellion* dollars"?) A lot of fashion styles come from rock stars and other media celebrities. (Have you ever worn your hair like Beyoncé or left your shirt unbuttoned like the guy in Blink 182?) Movies, too, provide ideas for trends to emulate. (Have you ever wanted a new pet after seeing the latest Disney flick or redecorated your room the way Hillary Duff's character did in her last show?) Remember, these styles and phrases were co-opted from you in the first place. So in a way, the media are selling your ideas back to you. The media are the example we're using to prove how easy it is to act on certain ideas. If *they* can do it (and the media are not as smart as you), *you* can do it, easy as pie. [If you don't know how to make pie, see p. 123.] Advertisers seem to think you have a *lot* of power over what your family and friends do. They rely on you to help make family decisions about purchases from breakfast cereal to cars, and they count on you to advertise to your friends. Why not use this power to your advantage?

The only trick to using this power is that you must have something you want people to do. You must develop a good idea for changing the world. You should identify a problem

15 Things That Are Wrong With Your World

(In Numerical Order)

1 _____

2 _____

3 _____

4 _____

5 _____

6 _____

7 _____

8 _____

9 _____

10 _____

11 _____

12 _____

13 _____

14 _____

15 _____

and try to create a solution. Maybe you already have one. If not, I can't tell you what you ideas will be, but I know they will be one *meeellion* times better than mine anyway.

The only way to be sure you will succeed in finding a solution is to find a problem that makes *your* life harder. If the issue you choose to work on affects you personally, you will never get bored of it or want to give up. There are probably lots of difficulties in your life. Are you no longer able to skateboard in a park in your neighborhood? Are you prohibited from wearing certain colors in school because of the administration's fear of gangs? Are you tired of the groups of mean boys that hang out and tease you in your neighborhood? Is your tap water clean enough to drink? Do you have a curfew or a bad babysitter or a really ugly sculpture on your block you need to get rid of? Are there adults in your neighborhood that creep you out? Also remember, even if stuff has been done before it is worth trying out your way.

These problems are all easily translatable into poetic solutions, or ways your world could be improved: change skateboarding restrictions in the park; help the administration find other ways to address gang issues in school; set up a neighborhood watch system made of people you trust that will be around if those mean boys start acting up; demand clean tap water from local officials; change the curfew, make sure the babysitter can't get work, or have that sculpture removed; and talk to other people about the adults that make you feel creepy.

But don't be afraid to take on something even bigger. If you don't already have something in mind, like leading a nationwide boycott against Smello™; creating a media exposé on the hidden dangers of Fasty-Drive™ advertisements; planning a protest about Crank Soda™'s use of sweatshops in their canning factories; making a fake VNR about MegaMedTech, Inc.'s painful LaserSaw™ machine; doing a scientific exposé about the toxic ingredients in Wah-Tir!™; planning a performance art event based on the PR misinformation that recently led us into war against Iraq; or creating a zine about how to live without ever buying another brand-name product again, don't worry. You'll get your own idea soon enough, and there are a lot more to consider in the rest of this book. Finish reading it before you give up your new evil scientist laugh.

When you settle on your own idea for changing the world (and you *will*), talk to your friends and family about it. Start with people you already know and trust, like a teacher who's really nice to you or an older sibling. Tell them your idea for improving the world and see how it goes. Find out if they'll help you work on your idea and talk to other people. Some people find talking about specific issues easier if they gather similar-minded folks together first, maybe by starting a club with rules and minutes and members and secret handshakes. Some people like joining groups that already exist. Other people would rather chat informally first.

Sometimes talking about problems can be enough, but most of the time, it's not. Try to talk about your idea with people in order to come up with something you can do that will help solve the problem. Share the problem as you see it and your ideas for a solution. (If the problem is that, following a recent hangnail epidemic in your neighborhood, no one on your block has a right hand anymore; your idea for a solution might be an informational pamphlet to teach people on other blocks about non-surgical options for hangnail treatment.) Be open-minded. Some people may not agree with you for very good reasons. (A man, for example, may love not having a right hand because he always hated writing letters.) Listen to constructive criticism and other ideas for solutions. (Maybe an informational brochure is a terrible idea, since it requires people with hangnails to hold a brochure, and they might not be able to because their hands are in such pain.) There might be better solutions out there. (Perhaps the lady across the street is willing to teach her parrot a short speech that can be delivered to the hangnail-afflicted.) If you don't settle on a solution right away, getting a few other people to understand what you want to change, and maybe to agree that *a* change is necessary, is a great first step. You can always settle on the perfect solution to the problem at the second meeting. Bwah-ha-ha-ha!

Try This at Home

Find something that bothers you for no apparent reason, like the color fuchsia, the letter "m," striped animals, tank tops, or strawberry flavoring. Make up some good, solid reasons why these things have a negative impact on the world. Then hold a meeting about it. If you serve chips and salsa, and keep the meeting short, everyone will come and stay through the whole thing. [Find recipes and instructions on p. 126.] Try to convince attendees of your point of view on this terrible color, this pointless pelt pattern, or this ridiculous fashion, flavor, or letter of the alphabet. Explain that the issues you raise are real and harmful. Use persuasive tactics, such as petitions, boycotts, rallies, and posters (more are described in a few pages), just for practice. Graphs can be helpful, too. Here are a few:

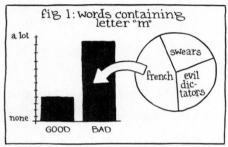

Fig. 1. Bar graph showing good versus bad words ("swears," French, names of evil dictators throughout history) containing the letter "m"

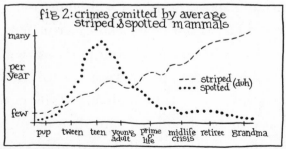

Fig. 2. Line graph comparing the number of spotted animals that lead lives of crime to the number of striped animals that lead lives of crime

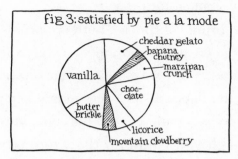

Fig. 3. Pie chart indicating percentage of satisfaction caused by various flavors of ice cream when paired with pie

If you can keep a straight face through the entire meeting, you may be able to have a serious debate about the issues you raise, which will be good practice for when you decide to hold a meeting about a serious, threatening issue. (Plus, you will have developed a reputation as someone who has fun meetings, so it'll be easier to get people to come the next time.)

Informing the Greater Community

Your next step will be to bring your idea—both the problem and your solution—to the greater community. Using examples from the past, here are a few ways to get your message across without ringing the doorbells of every single person who shops at your grocery store and goes to the same movie theater you do (although you could do that, too). [See p. 130 for tips on being polite.]

Boycotts

An extremely traditional political activity invented in Ireland, a boycott is when a group of people refuse to purchase products from or patronize a company in order to enforce a change in the company's practices. Although abstaining from spending money is a key element in boycotting, the more significant work is describing your reasons for not spending money and articulating your demands for change. Also note that a boycott must be held by a group, and cannot be performed by an individual—the larger the group, the faster your demands will be heard. Boycotts can be initial elements of political action. United Students

Against Sweatshops (USAS), for example, was formed when students realized collegiate apparel is a $2.5 billion industry—an industry with factories using ridiculously unfair labor practices. One USAS activist told journalist Liza Featherstone in her book *Students Against Sweatshops,* "The system is completely dependent on us going out and spending money on all this crap!" Although they do take time to build support, boycotts can be very successful as in the case of the Boycott Nestlé campaign created in response to the infant fatalities we discussed in the last chapter. [See "Planning a Boycott," p. 162.]

Demonstrations and rallies

Most political organizations hold demonstrations or rallies as a way of showing support for ideas or issues. The Immigrant Workers Freedom Ride held a nationwide bus tour in the summer of 2003 to demonstrate the struggle for economic and social justice and civil rights for America's most marginalized population—immigrants. Buses from Seattle, Los Angeles, San Francisco, Houston, Chicago, Boston, Miami, Las Vegas, Portland, and Minneapolis traveled 20,000 miles of highway to show support for the 16 million undocumented workers in the United States. The Freedom Riders felt that racist policies similar to those that kicked off the original Freedom Rides in 1961 are damaging the lives of these undocumented U.S. residents. The Immigrant Workers Freedom Ride, supported by a broad coalition of organizations and individuals (including unions, businesses, students, and others), regularly held traditional protests during stops along their tour and integrated activities such as competitive sing-a-longs and puppetry into their demands for equality. Lately, however, people have also used demonstrations to make a point about public space. Some people are frustrated that public space disappears rapidly when it is covered in logos or sold off to private owners. Reclaim the Streets, an organization that started in the U.K., is a loose, international network of groups that hold similar goals and throw similar parties. They aim to use urban streets to make a political point about private messages (like advertising) in public spaces (like on billboards). They believe people who stay inside all the time don't know or care about the larger society. Whether or not these parties are legal depends on local laws and if the organizers get permits to hold demonstrations. [See "Having Fun," p. 129, "Papier Maché," p. 162, and tips for holding a meeting on p. 132.]

Educational Programming

Teach-ins and public speakers were popular in the anti–Vietnam war movement in the 1960s, and feminists of the 1970s held consciousness-raising sessions during which they shared personal experiences, at which some women learned, often for the first time, that some of their most frustrating experiences were quite common. Currently, Educating for Justice, Inc. is an organization that develops, produces and distributes justice-oriented educational programming and content through the web, films, educational events, and publishing. Headed by Jim Keady, a former professional soccer player with the New Jersey Imperials and a former college coach. After being fired for refusing to wear Nike's products as part of the school's $3.5 million dollar endorsement deal with the sportswear giant, Keady immersed himself in the lives of sweatshop workers in Indonesia, founded Educating for Justice, and became a lead campaigner of the group's Stop Nike Sweatshops campaign. Generally speaking, education is a legal activity in the U.S., although teachers and writers regularly get into trouble for teaching the wrong things. (Don't worry about getting into trouble yourself, just be glad whenever teachers tell you anything genuinely useful.)

Graffiti, Stencils, and Billboard Manipulations

Since the 1970s, the Billboard Liberation Front in San Francisco has been using elaborate graphic design techniques to manipulate certain well-known billboard ads. A neon sign for Camel cigarettes, for example, was changed to read "Am I Dead Yet?" The organization uses advertising that already exists in popular public places to spread messages about corporations. This kind of work is illegal (it's called "defamation" or "vandalism") and participants risk arrest when they manipulate billboards. The alterations also create extra work for the laborers who put up the billboards, so the Billboard Liberation Front tries to leave presents for the workers who come to tear down the "liberated" billboard. [See p. 138 for information about laws.] Graffiti, tagging, bombing, and stenciling—paintings done in public space usually by underground individuals or small artists' groups—are also illegal, despite the beautiful images produced and the high degree of skill needed to complete them. [See "Stencils," p. 164.]

Mocking Public Figures

The Biotic Baking Brigade (based in San Francisco) throws pies at people whose politics the group disagrees with, like in old comedy movies. They—and other pastry-based activists throughout the world—demand that specific, identifiable people be held responsible for large corporate and governmental acts of atrocity. They try to match the flavor of the pie with the crimes of the targets, so their message can be understood on many levels. Clare Short, Britain's International Development Secretary and a Governor of the World Bank, was pied by an organization called Just Dessert. Short was struck with a confection made of fair-trade bananas and local organic ingredients to dramatize her mistreatment of the world's poor. Pie-slinging antics are pretty funny, although they have also been called assault, which is a crime. The *Onion*, a weekly satirical newspaper, also mocks public figures (under the protection of laws allowing satire), but primarily for entertainment. Similar parodies have been created countless times by various groups to call attention to serious issues in a humorous way. [See p. 123 for pie recipes and "Having Fun," p. 129.]

Pirate Radio and Internet Broadcasting

Art-noise band Negativland creates sound-based pranks and projects to make statements about our consumer culture. Recently, the group forced a Seattle-based Clear Channel (the largest owner of radio stations in the world) affiliate to change its radio playlist. Perhaps a minor victory, the prank did prove that goofy projects can have serious impact. The joke started a year and a half earlier, when the group was invited to contribute to "Reclaim the Media," an event scheduled to coincide with (and protest) the 2002 National Association of Broadcasters convention, a gathering that favored media conglomerates like Clear Channel. KJR-FM, a local station claiming to play "The Greatest Hits of the '60s and '70s," was the prank's target. In fact, the station also played hits from the 1980s, so Negativland accused KJR-FM and Clear Channel of false advertising. Negativland created a character called DJ Diekobiscz (pronounced *Dick*-o-bitch) and aired his crazed ranting as a fake KJR deejay over pirated radio stations surrounding the actual KJR-FM. Many listeners tuned in by accident, thinking they were listening to a real deejay. The tape loop played on several stations throughout the 2002 broadcaster convention/"Reclaim the Media" weekend. Then in the late summer of 2003, visitors to Negativland's website were able to hear the tape loop online. An Internet message board took up the cause and drew supporters. Following a wave of complaining emails, Clear Channel reformed the KJR-FM playlist. While pirate radio stations are only legal if they broadcast within a small range, some activists use transportable equipment to escape detection. If you have access to it, the Internet, which is much less regulated, can be a cheaper and easier way of doing your thing. Just make sure people know to listen!

15 Ideas for Solving the Things That Are Wrong with Your World (In Numerical Order)

1 _____

2 _____

3 _____

4 _____

5 _____

6 _____

7 _____

8 _____

9 _____

10 _____

11 _____

12 _____

13 _____

14 _____

15 _____

Posters, flyers, and stickers

When feminists first started looking at advertising and identifying sexism, they created stickers that read, "This ad is demeaning toward women." Feminists who didn't like the underlying message of an ad simply pasted a sticker on it. That way people looking at the ad would find an immediate, visual reminder that the underlying message in the ad deserved closer inspection. Antiwar messages were spread this way during the 2003 Iraq War, many having to do with things President Bush lied about. My favorite sticker simply states "BUSH LIED" in black and white (I got mine from the folks at *Clamor*). It's a simple message, but visually and intellectually arresting. In addition to stickers, people also create posters and flyers to spread messages, to attract attention to events, and to provide information for campaigns. The legality of posting and distributing these depends on where you live and how or where you put up your work. [See "Graphic Design," p. 147 and "The Law," p. 138.]

Street Theater and Performances

The Pink Bloque in Chicago goes to large, pre-organized, traditional protests in matching pink outfits, performs choreographed dances to popular music, and teaches the public their moves. By doing so, they enlist people to show support for their cause. This is effective because some people are more likely to dance than they are to march around screaming things they might not have had time to consider. The dances are usually legal because they are held during other demonstrations for which the organizers have acquired proper permits. Dances in dissent held separate from demonstrations sometimes bring the police, but since a part of the Pink Bloque's political tactic is to act cute and flirtatious, they are rarely arrested. Similarly, the Infernal Noise Brigade in Seattle combines percussion instruments, majorettes, marching, rifle-twirling, and crazy costumes with carnival-like insurrection. They crash demonstrations and other people's concerts, or make random street appearances to, for example, protest adults who spend too much time in bars. (This sort of loud political action does often bring the police.) Puppetry has also become a very popular form of fun, issue-based street theater, as you may have noticed in pictures from most major protests of the last few years. Reverend Billy of the Church of Stop Shopping in New York combines theater, protests, and boycotts to "preach" to Disney Store shoppers and Starbucks customers about those companies' reliance on underpaid workers, unsafe factory conditions, and cruel, monopolistic methods of expansion. [See "Research," p. 135.]

Striking

Kids as young as eleven planned amazing school walkouts in protest of the 2003 Iraq War. Student strikes throughout Europe, Australia, and the U.S. were central to antiwar protests. Youngsters bravely faced violence and attempts to stop their right to protest by school authorities, local police, and national governments. While the walkouts held consequences for students such as suspension, expulsion from school, or even arrest for truancy, students participated nonetheless. Some students were locked in school buildings or guarded with police dogs when they tried to participate. Striking is not illegal, keep in mind, but it is considered unsupportive of the ruling government, which can be just as bad as being against the law. [For information on organizing people, see p. 130. See p. 138 for information on the law.] One group of students released a press statement outlining the reasons for their protest and a short list of demands they felt would ease U.S.-Iraqi tensions immediately. These two small pieces of propaganda were effective and useful, as they provided members of the press with a very clear explanation of the students' reasons for walking out of class. The media was not able to claim, for example, that these kids walked out just to go hang out at the beach. [To get tips on writing a press release, see p. 150.]

Zines and Self-Publishing

Since the late 1960s, small, self-published books and pamphlets have been created in people's basements, on jobs when the boss is away, in schools, and at Kinko's as a way of producing media. Artists, writers, and publishers frustrated with and rejected by mainstream media figured out another way to put their work in the public eye. Zines have been created, quite literally, on all imaginable topics. *Temp*

Slave! explores the vast world of temporary office workers; *Doris*, a personal zine, combines drawing and writing to tell intimate but extremely educational stories; *Hip Mama* is a resource for radical parents and educators; *Dishwasher* describes one man's attempt to hold jobs washing dishes in every state; *Cometbus*, another personal zine, relates one punk's belief system and adventures; *Xtra Tuf*, distributed free to commercial fisherwomen, narrates tales from that unique world; and *Bitch*, *Punk Planet*, *Bust*, and many other currently popular magazines all started as small, self-published zines. Zines have explored radical distribution methods, innovative design techniques, and copyright issues. Some have expanded the traditional notion of literature; others explore radical notions of body image and self-esteem; some provide very simple instructions on helpful or amusing topics like living a vegan lifestyle or stealing office supplies from your day job. Zines are given away at concerts or events, found for free in bathrooms or on sale at independent bookstores, or are stumbled across by accident. (One zine, intended for gas-station attendants, was strapped to the gas cap of vehicles in states where station attendants pump all gas by law. Vehicle owners likely never even knew they were distributing activist literature!) Personally, I have created zines on topics including pie, Starbucks, local newspaper the *Seattle Times*, and the importance of people named Anne. Just about everything you read in this book was originally tested as a zine. I may be biased, but I believe there's no limit to what can be done when you combine your creative interests with your desire to change the world.

Some of these ideas are pretty exciting, and others likely seem boring. Everyone's heard of the Boston Tea Party, when a bunch of white people dressed up like Indians a zillion years ago and dumped tea into the harbor to protest taxation, but have you really put much thought into what a protest like that would involve? It was probably very exciting to participate in, even though it sounds lame as hell in your history book. Remember, the way political actions are represented might not sound like fun because of who is telling you about it: usually, it's the media. They may have reasons for making it sound *not* fun. For example, the protests they describe may be against something they support.

You may not be able to change the world by simply telling people about your great idea; you may have to learn to participate in the democratic process and change the legal system. Legislation may be difficult for young adults to influence since you can't yet vote, but you can advocate for specific changes to laws and convince adults that your cause is vital for young people.

Doesn't it make more sense for you to change a law regulating public concerts, copyright use, pirate radio, graffiti, or skateboarding than to get arrested for it? It might take longer, but if you're going to change the world, you may as well do it right.

Try This at Home

Change a law. I'm not kidding. It doesn't have to be a big one, and it doesn't have to be a federal one. Just find a stupid law and get rid of it. There are many dumb laws out there, and a disproportionate number of them probably affect you, so it will be easy to find one you don't like. If you like the democratic process, *A Kids Guide to Social Action* by Barbara Lewis or *So You Want to Make a Difference:*

15 Projects You Can Do to Implement Your Solutions for Things That Are Wrong with Your World

(In Numerical Order)

1 _____

2 _____

3 _____

4 _____

5 _____

6 _____

7 _____

8 _____

9 _____

10 _____

11 _____

12 _____

13 _____

14 _____

15 _____

Advocacy Is the Key by Nancy Amidei can give you more information on using it effectively. [See Appendix G.]

Tell the World How You're Changing It

You've planned your boycott, copied your zine, and changed all the dumb laws in your town. Now you have to let people know what you've done, or they won't be able to help you out. There are three different methods for getting your ideas out to the wider public: one, you can sway mainstream media; two, you can change existing media to suit your message; or three, you can make your own media.

Mainstream media means the very few, very large companies that control most of what we experience on television, in print, and on the Internet or the radio. Specifically these include: Time Warner, General Electric, Viacom, Disney, Liberty Media Corporation, AT&T, News Corporation, Bertelsmann, Vivendi Universal, and Sony. It won't be too difficult for you to sway these companies. You know advertisers love you, and you know what mainstream media like: kidz and money!

One way to have a say in what the media do is to work for one of these companies. You might even be able to get an internship immediately. While a job like this can be financially rewarding, remember that change from the inside takes a long time. It can be frustrating for people who like to change things quickly. Plus, by the time you are in a position to change anything, you may have grown comfortable with the way things are.

You can also simply use mainstream media for what they offer: catchy, attractive news items, exciting headlines, and vapid entertainment. Get interviewed on the nightly news, send your press release to the paper, or record your pop song. Just remember: the media have their own agendas. You won't be able to change them, no matter how popular or long your song, story, or interview turns out to be.

Other people take existing media and change it for their own purposes, like the Billboard Liberation Front and the early feminists. This is sometimes called "culture jamming," a term invented by Negativland but adopted by the magazine *Adbusters*. If you choose to make use of existing media for your own purposes (called "appropriating media"), remember the Rule of Logos: if people see what looks like a real logo, they will perceive your appropriation as an advertisement. Be careful what media you use. Appropriating media can take many forms. You can re-edit a TV sitcom to tell a new story or make a collage about racism in teen magazines for your bedroom. You can audiotape your classmates singing commercial jingles during recess or make a documentary video with your friends about the documentary video you had to watch in health class. Sometimes the mainstream media get very picky about copyright issues, but sometimes, since they know about the Rule of Logos too, they don't care. They just think you're helping them advertise. Fortunately, copyright laws are some of the dumbest laws around. Maybe you should get rid of them before you decide to appropriate existing media.

There is, however, a third option for telling the world how you're going to change it: make your own media. In some ways, this is the easiest method of getting your message out to the public because no one can tell you how to do it and it's basically legal. On the other hand, it's extremely difficult because it takes an amazing amount of energy and resources. Fortunately, you should be able to find all the resources you need in the Ways and Means section. The energy you can get from eating pie.

Try This at Home

Find a creative way to "reuse" an ad. Choose an ad from a fast food bag, a poster, a magazine, or from a commercial or a product placement spot on TV or in a movie. Use the same medium as the original ad to create an alternative. In your new version, try to discern the real, hidden message of the original ad. An ad for hairspray that tells you how much "hold" the spray has could actually be saying that girls need to spend more time attracting boys and less time thinking about important world economic matters. An ad trying to sell you athletic clothing may actually be trying to convince you that you are overweight, although the makers of the ad have never met you and probably never will. An ad for a burger joint may be selling you the idea of an extremely unhealthy lifestyle, not just greasy fast food. Make a new spoof ad that resembles the old ad but that clearly states the hidden message in the ad. If you are feeling brave, put it in a place where people usually view ads. See if anyone notices. If people ask about it tell them it's a new, edgy campaign. (In a way, it is!)

6. WAYS AND MEANS

You're all fired up now to make some sort of cultural statement or product, but you're still not sure *how*. This chapter will show you. It's divided into five sections: Working with People, Collecting Information, Gathering Resources, Getting the Word Out, and Your Project. This book won't answer all your questions, but it might help you figure out the right ones to ask, and it may help you stay sane while you're figuring it all out. Adults, please note: the kids reading this book are your best resource. Find out what they want to change and help them. Do it their way. I'm sorry to tell you this, but they are probably smarter than you are.

What's the most important thing you would tell a young adult interested in initiating an activist project?

Start small, but don't be afraid to think big. Imagine what the project would look like if it were completely successful.
—*Joshua Breitbart (29), Allied Media Projects*

Understand that while you may feel alone, you are not.
—*Rachel (28), The Pink Bloque*

Educate people first! Many students who reach the point of wanting to be "activists" sometimes forget that there was once a point in their lives when they didn't have a clue about social issues. Don't ever forget that and always consider it when you head off to change the world. In order for you to gain support for your campaign/issue, you have to deliver information to people in a way that they can easily understand it, that engages them and leaves

Working with People
Feeding People

It is amazing what people will do for you if you know how to cook. A good cook uses sharp knives and hot surfaces, so if you need assistance, get someone to help you! It is not cool to burn or cut yourself, and it is extra not cool to burn down a building or cut someone else. Please do not do these things.

Most activists will tell you the most important thing you can have on hand for any organizing effort is **coffee**. In a recent informal poll, 100 percent of everyone I talked to told me they wouldn't take an informal poll unless I made them coffee. The best way to make coffee is to measure it. Put a filter in the basket of the coffeemaker. Do not use a smelly sock for a filter. Add one tablespoon of coffee per cup of water and one extra tablespoon of coffee ("for the pot," people say) and then pour the correct amount of water into the coffeemaker. Turn on the coffeemaker and wait patiently for it to finish brewing, then serve. If you don't drink coffee, good for you! If you do drink it, don't drink it every day. Don't get addicted to caffeine. Bad coffee can taste like ashy mud, and you do not want to have to drink it just to get your fix.

If you don't want to make coffee, you can make a **pie**. People will do anything for pie. In some ways, pie is better than coffee because it seems harder to make but isn't. Also you can "pie" someone (like the Biotic Baking Brigade does) if you know how to make a pie, but you can't "coffee" anyone without burning them (which is mean and illegal).

Start with the crust. (Store-bought crusts are terrible and expensive.) Throw three cups of flour in a bowl and salt lightly. Cut in 2/3 of a cup of shortening. (This is basically a glob of fat. You can use butter if you prefer, but butter is also basically a glob of fat.) Use the backside of a fork to "cut in" the shortening (that means,

physical, spiritual, economic, personal, intellectual.
—*Evon Peter (27), Native Movement*

Believe in your ideas but try to understand where others' ideas come from.
—*Dara (32), The Pink Bloque*

Don't think of "activism" as a special thing to which you devote some part of your time. Make it a part of your every day life. . . . Every decision you will make every day will have an impact on others, so ask if the decisions you are making are revolutionizing your planet or replicating the worst parts of the status quo. In the INB, we're musicians and performers, so music and performance are a big part of our "activism," but we also try to practice gender equity in dating relationships, education by reading books, and environmentalism by driving as little as possible. These underlying ethics that we hold are not just some external political

philosophy to address at the level of government, but ideally, are guidelines for daily life.
—The Professor (31), The Infernal Noise Brigade

Whatever you do, do it with all your heart and don't hold back. Magic happens when you commit yourself to be a positive force in this wounded world.
—Agent Apple, Biotic Baking Brigade

Know your facts better than the opposition.
—Wendy Talley (41), The Spot Youth Center

Pick a subject you care deeply about. Don't try to save the world with your first project. Just make it modest enough so you can get it done, considering your resources at the moment and—most important—have a sense of humor about it and yourself.
—Robbie Conal, guerrilla postering activist

break the shortening into small, flour-coated pieces), or if you want to get fancy, use a device called a pastry cutter. It's shaped like several metal *U*'s stacked together and secured with a handle. Add a spoonful or two of ice-cold water. Mash it all together gently to keep your crust light. When you have a good, dry consistency (dry crusts are good) sprinkle a flat surface with flour. Also rub your rolling pin with flour and put some flour on your shirt, so everyone will know you made the pie from scratch. Roll out the dough and place the flattened crust carefully into the pie pan, or mash it in with your hands if you are short on time. Squish together any holes in your crust. If you need extra dough to patch holes, trim the edges hanging over the pie plate.

To make the filling, take some fruit—any fruit! I made pie once with out-of-date fruit cocktail from a can!—and peel it if it has a peel. (Except probably don't peel grapes. In fact, don't make a grape pie at all. Grody.) Chop the fruit up if it's too big to fit into your mouth. Put the fruit into a bowl with a little flour or corn-starch to thicken the juice, cinnamon (and maybe also cloves, nutmeg, ginger, vanilla extract, butter, or coconut shavings), and some kind of sweetener. (I have used honey, brown sugar, white sugar, and Britney Spears CDs. But be careful: too much sugar will make your pie soupy.) Mix it all up and pour into the crust. If you want a top crust, you can either make it the exact same way as you made the bottom crust (use cookie-cutters to make shapes or overlay alternating thins strips to make a latticework crust if you want to impress people), or you can throw some butter, brown sugar, and flour into a bowl, mix it up together, and dump it over the top of your pie. When it bakes it will turn deli-cious and melty and anyone who eats it will be under your control for an hour.

Don't be intimidated by the assumption that there is a *right* way to do things. It is possible to create change and organize community using the resources we have available to us, i.e. photocopied publications (zines), graffiti and public art, basements turned into meeting spaces, benefit shows that highlight our communities' talent—allow yourself to feel that you are a part of a move-ment and create active communities that support each other and are com-mitted to social change, rather than feeling like it's your duty to *save* someone else.
—*Nomy Lamm (28), writer, performer, and community organizer*

125

Bake your pie at 350°F for about forty minutes. Hang out in the kitchen while it's cooking because you do not want a burned pie. A burned pie is a crime against humanity. Put leftover dough on a cookie sheet, sprinkle with cinnamon and sugar, and bake for five minutes. These pie tasties can be eaten while you are waiting for the real pie to cool.

Now that you know how to make coffee and pie, let's move on to **salsa**, that way if anyone comes along with a bag of tortilla chips you'll know how to make a complete meal. Salsa is just as easy as pie, but with more vegetables. Also, most people believe it should be consumed before pie, although this is debatable.

Chop tomatoes, green peppers, onions, garlic, and cilantro. It's okay to ask people in the grocery store to show you these things if you don't know what they are. If you wanna get seriously radical, start an organic garden and grow this stuff yourself. But if you're short on time, just go to the store. Sometimes it's more important to be stress-free than it is to be radical.

Toss your ingredients and a pinch of salt into a bowl and mix. If you want, experiment by adding pineapple, peaches, tomatillos, green or red onions, carrot shavings, red or orange peppers, corn, black beans, jalepeño or habeñero peppers, lime or lemon juice, or apricots. These all make delicious salsas and will help you win people over. Serve with chips, on burgers, over tortillas or heat-and-serve burritos, in soup, or eat it plain for breakfast if you are a weirdo. To make guacamole, add your salsa to some mushed-up, ripe avocados.

Late-night gatherings may be a good time to serve **tea (mint and ginger)**. Find mint plants in your neighborhood and pick them, or purchase some ginger at the store. It is cheap and looks like a tulip bulb or dried femur. Let fresh-picked mint dry for a few days, and then pour boiling water over it to make tea. Mint tea

to respect those, but you can also expect people to work hard and do what they say they're going to do. For yourself, you need to understand your own limitations and only commit to doing what you can actually accomplish. . . . Cooperation beats competition every time.
—*Joshua Breitbart (29), Allied Media Projects*

We all have our strengths and weaknesses. Work with peoples' strengths rather than focusing on their weaknesses and do the same with yourself. Ask for help when you need it or when someone else can do something more efficiently and effectively.
—*Evon Peter (27), Native Movement*

Learning to listen. okay, this is different for everyone, but it's learning that the concerns of others are as important to them as your concerns are to you. Forget objectivity. If someone thinks they are hurting, they are. It's hard to step out of our own narrow perspectives long enough to realize this,

but if we do, it is also the most rewarding experience.
—*The Professor (31), The Infernal Noise Brigade*

Making decisions with groups of people takes a lot more time than making decisions by yourself—but the time it takes is made up for by the relationships you build through the process.
—*Dara (32), The Pink Bloque*

is good for soothing nerves and calming upset tummies. Ginger can be sliced up thinly and boiled for tea, or you can combine the dried mint and the sliced ginger for ginger-mint tea. Ginger tea is good for getting the brain working, and ginger-mint tea just tastes delicious.

General Health and Safety

When using chemicals (like paint!) or working with sick people, wear gloves and a mask. Get enough sleep, even though you might not have finished changing the world yet. Eat healthy, and eat in a way that conforms to your politics. (Sorry! No more fast food if you're working on anti-globalization issues, and no more meat if you join up with PETA.) Exercise. Avoid falling off cliffs. Do not eat poison. Wear a full suit of armor if you even have to look at a knife.

Having Fun

Have fun every single moment you're working. Do things just because they're silly and because you can. Don't be too surprised if you start catching the media in more and more lies after you've read this book, but also don't let this depress you. Learn to find it funny. Knowing the media are lying to you just means you're smart, and that is no reason to be bummed out. If you aren't happy changing the world, don't do it. Changing the world requires too much work, energy, and time to do if it's not any fun. By the same token, work only with good fun people you respect and enjoy, but work with them a lot once you locate them.

Manners and Appearance

No matter what anyone tries to tell you, there is no uniform for being political or artistic. That being said, certain types of dress elicit certain reactions, and knowing these can help you achieve your goals. The importance of black **clothes**, you will soon discover, is not only that others recognize you as "artistic," but also that you can spill all over yourself and no one will notice. Occasionally, *not* wearing black clothes can be a good way to make people think you are cheery, well-adjusted, and in favor of the status quo, which can be helpful in political organizing. Sometimes, the best way to make your important political point will be to wear a baby blue bunny suit. Other kids may make fun of you (other adults make fun of me all the time), but they would probably do that no matter what you wore.

More important than what you wear is being **polite**. Good manners are activism's secret weapon. Being polite will get you far in this world, but never compromise on what you want—just learn to ask for it nicely and repeat yourself if you must. Yes, it's archaic to say please and thank you and would you perchance consider passing the butter, but it works. Use it. Overdo it. Please?

Organizing People

A good leader is effective at **delegating tasks and responsibilities**. If you learn this skill quickly, and learn it well, you will never be frustrated with other people.

Delegating responsibilities can be simple, as long as you do it exactly as I describe here:

Make a list of all the tasks that need to get done to complete a certain project.

Bring this list to your group's next meeting.

Assign people tasks they are good at and will enjoy. Write each person's name next to every task you assign.

Assume everyone will do the tasks they agree to do, but offer any and all assistance you can along the way. Together, set a deadline for the completion of the task and make sure the person responsible knows why that deadline was chosen and what it is.

Do all the unassigned tasks on the list. Those are the only ones you are responsible for. Do them well. Never feel bad or responsible for someone else not doing something. If you have delegated a task or responsibility, it is not yours to worry about. Take the time you would usually spend fretting about other people to make yourself a delicious pie.

131

Activists like **meetings**, but many don't know how to hold a productive one. The first step to holding a successful meeting is making sure it is necessary. If you are drowning in the bathtub, for example, and need help, a meeting wouldn't be the best way of getting your message across. If multiple things need to be discussed and decided upon, however, a meeting may be necessary. Keep all meetings under an hour. If it is an extremely important meeting, it can go to an hour and a half. Write out an agenda of what you will discuss before the meeting and get it to everyone before they arrive. Do not allow chit-chat or gossip at the meeting—tell people to hang out and talk after the meeting, when you are done with business. If people go off topic, remind them to stick to the agenda so you can be done with the meeting fast. If something takes too long, stop discussing it and put it on the agenda for the next meeting. People who come to meetings should expect to leave with a list of things to do before the next meeting, and they should all be willing to describe briefly what they have done since the last meeting. After the meeting go eat pizza or something and spend a lot of time talking about what a great meeting that was.

Prejudice

Examine yourself, your ideas, and the people you work with for sexism, racism, classism, and other prejudices. This is not difficult, just think hard about what you care about and why. If you find that you care about something, but don't really know why, research it a little more. Prejudice is sneaky—like advertising—because it makes us *feel* certain ways without any good reasons. Eliminate prejudice wherever you can, or find a way to use it to your advantage. For example, sexism is a fact of our culture: society believes women are dumber, quieter, and less engaged in world events than men, so the media, the police, local business owners, and your neighbors will often either be surprised or refuse to believe it when girls speak up or act out. Smart boys will realize they could use this gap in social awareness by actively recruiting girls to their causes and giving them positions of great power. Smart girls, how-

Where would you advise a young adult to search for interesting, unbiased information?

Interview multiple generations, conduct focus groups, and look in their hearts.
—*Wendy Talley (41), The Spot Youth Center*

All information is biased. It just depends on what type of filter it is coming through. Given this, I suggest that people check out a range of publications across the spectrum of political persuasions as well as professional backgrounds. For example, I am currently heavily focused on the sweatshop issue. So that I am as informed as I can be on this, I read commentaries from workers, activists, lawyers, businesspeople, ethicists, theologians, philosophers, educators, etc. The greater your base of information, the better prepared you will be to educate people about the issue you care about. Remember, your opinion on an issue is only as good as the information

ever, are probably already busy working on their own things and causes.

Smoking and Drinking

Don't do either, even if everyone you like does. Why? These are bad, unhealthy habits, and someday when you run out of cigarettes you will be very, very unhappy. Why put yourself through that? Don't bother starting. Remaining addiction-free (this includes caffeine!) is a safe, easy way of staying happy, healthy, and sane, even when you're working really hard.

Collecting Information
Notes

Constant **note-taking** is vital to activism. You should take notes on anything of interest to you at all. Hopefully, unless you checked it out of the library, this book is already filled with underlining and margin notes. (It's your book, after all. Don't let anyone tell you any different.) Many people carry around notebooks for this exact reason. Some carry around small tape-recorders .(Andy Warhol called his taperecorder his "wife.") Certain people have even replaced themselves with exact robot duplicates that visually and aurally record everything they experience, so nothing can ever be forgotten through human error. (Actually, I think I dreamed that. Sorry.) It doesn't matter if you think you are good at taking notes or if you are trying to write down everything word-for-word. As long as you are putting something on paper (or tape or Robotic Memory System), it will be helpful later.

Research

Back up your opinions with facts. Read books, articles, and web sites on topics that

you have to back it up. So do your homework!
—*Jim Keady, Educating for Justice, Inc.*

In the library, bookstores, Pacifica Radio, not-for-profit news outlets, the Internet. Science. But I must say this . . . it is almost impossible to find material devoid of bias.
—*Janeane Garofalo (39), activist, comedian, and actor*

I would advise people to look for truth in individual people's stories and experiences. Foster relationships, read first-hand accounts, look for perspectives that aren't represented in the media. Check sites like indymedia.org. Be open to different perspectives. Learn by observing.
—*Nomy Lamm (28), writer, performer, and community organizer*

Don't believe the corporate media claims of being objective. To find interesting information, go to a local independent bookstore if there's one near you.
—*Agent Apple, Biotic Baking Brigade*

interest you and watch videos on these topics for fun. Start with those listed in **Appendices A through D**.

If you have web access, **online research** is very easy. I start with Google (google.com). Here's how it works: In the blank box in the middle of the screen, type in some words that relate to your research project, and then click "Google Search." Start with the obvious phrases: mad cow disease, advertising in public schools, girls' body images, or tropical rain forest. You don't need to type in a complete sentence. You can type in seemingly unrelated words and see what comes up: cannibalism recipe, cat-hair fashion statement, or cancer-causing playground equipment. Several links will come up. Read through a few of them and note the best ones to check again later. Remember, the Rule of Logos even applies to websites. Be careful what information you take in; just because the Internet provides a *lot* of information doesn't mean any of it is accurate.

Interviews are excellent research tools. People that are willing to talk to you directly can provide a wide range of information, as well as ideas for gathering more information. (A good final question for all interviews is, "How can I find out more about the things you've told me?") Almost anyone is available for an informational interview if you ask them to talk to you and remain polite. Take notes!

The addresses listed in **Appendix E** are provided for you to make use of in whatever way you desire. Send these people copies of your CDs, questionnaires, press releases, or just invite them over for a piece of pie so you can discuss matters personally. These people are so-called powerful people in our society, but you should realize by now that you're just as powerful as they are (although you probably don't have as much money). When you write to them, say hi for me.

Research can be tricky if you do not know what you are looking for. In the interest of saving you a little time, **Appendix F** lists a number of media corporations and some of their holdings. Although you may not be interested in

What resources would you advise youth to look to for inspiration?

The ACLU and the National Lawyers' Guild are great legal resources if you're planning anything that involves civil disobedience.
—*Robbie Conal, guerrilla postering activist*

I think Derrick Jensen's *A Language Older than Words* is the book that comes the closest to representing the values that I try to live by, and the place that my activism comes from. It's a rough book; it's basically about all the scariest things in the world (child abuse, genocide, racism, environmental destruction) but its power is in its compassion and integrity, its commitment to opening up space for the voices that are being throttled. Probably not appropriate for all young people, as I could see it being potentially traumatizing if you're not in a space to be able to absorb it—nonetheless it's changed a lot of people's lives and I think it's an

directly taking on an issue related to the media or media representations, it can be helpful to know who is behind harmful or counterproductive images, resources, or websites. Even if you aren't influenced by the media, remember, almost everyone else is.

The Law

Research the law in your area. Get to know a cool lawyer and ask her or him about what you want to do before you do it. Consult the American Civil Liberties Union (ACLU) and the National Lawyers Guild. [See Appendix C for web sites.] Many states have free legal advice for artists, listed on the Internet as "lawyers for the creative arts," "legal art clinics," or something similar. Ask your social studies teacher to help locate someone or ask for class credit when you locate a lawyer on your own.

Gathering Resources
Money

Make some fast **seed money** to start your project by organizing a bake sale, running a lemonade stand, holding a carwash (use biodegradable soap or you will pollute water and kill fish), or having a band throw you a benefit concert (where they play and charge money at the door and you get to keep it in exchange for food and publicity). You could also busk (play an instrument or do a performance on the street corner for donations—be sure to tell people what you're doing with the money!), sell stuff you made (maybe online), do yard work, or baby-sit (this also gives you helpers).

Ask for **grant money** from organizations you know or already work with, maybe the Boys and Girls Club, Girl or Boy Scouts, YMCA, YWCA, Rotary Club, the Jewish Community Center, or other organizations. You might want

important resource to know about.
—*Nomy Lamm (28), writer, performer, and community organizer*

Read all the classics, even those that support the things in our world you don't like. You can't critique and change the monster if you don't understand it.
—*The Professor (31), The Infernal Noise Brigade*

Intern or join social justice organizations just to learn from older people. When you figure out what you do and don't like about existing groups or organizations, organize your own with your friends!
—*Dara (32), The Pink Bloque*

to consider writing grant proposals to people you know as well as to grant making organizations like these. Sitting down and writing your ideas out for what you want to do with money you get from your uncle may convince him to really fork it over. You might find it's easier to locate funding for specific projects—like making a series of antiwar posters on hand-made paper—than to get funded for the establishment of a committee or a series of phone calls. People like to give money to visual projects that are creative but professionally presented and easy to accomplish. Presenting your project this way may make it easier to find funding.

Below is a sample outline you can use when a grant provider does not provide a form to fill out, or when you are writing a grant proposal to someone you know. Remember the most important thing in grant writing is proving that you want to and know how to do your project. Although many grant makers require you to fill out their forms, some do not. If they do, use their forms and read the directions *twice*. When you're writing a grant, always have someone else read it over before you turn it in.

Your name. Add your age and a guardian's name if you are under 18.

Your project. In three to five detailed sentences describe your project. Use the names of other people and their credentials wherever you can. Try to make your project sound fancy and professional although it might not really be.

Budget. List everything you need to buy to make your project happen and its cost, including food for volunteers, supplies, staple-guns, pie ingredients, black fabric remnants, tape, postage—*everything*. Also list everything you already have or will get donated for free, except instead of cost, list it as a donation. Total this up, and subtract from it money you already have for the project. This will be your total. Make sure you are asking for that amount. In the sample budget below, for example, you are asking for $75 and investing $15 of your own money.

Sample $75 grant budget for a pro-homeschooling collage shown on telephone poles throughout your city:

A billion thumbtacks	$27.00
Old newspapers	Donation (from recycling center)
Food for big collage party	$50.00
Glue and tape	$13.00
SUBTOTAL:	$90
Personal investment	$15
TOTAL AMOUNT NEEDED: $75	

Statement of purpose. In a paragraph, describe why you are doing your project in terms of its greater social impact. Explain how it will affect participants, various communities, and the viewers of the final project. Mention research information like newspaper articles or book titles if you want to sound like a super pro.

Raw Materials

Research organizations in your neighborhood that donate supplies to youth-led programs, or try to work through a Boys and Girls Club, YMCA, YWCA, Rotary

Club, the Jewish Community Center, or other organizations, as these all have access to more people and materials than you will find on your own. Need paint? Ask a paint store. Need sporting goods? Call a gym, a local sports team, or a famous athlete. The two tricks to getting donations are asking nicely and thanking profusely.

Getting the Word Out

Send press releases, media kits, and letters of intent; post flyers, make telephone calls, announce your plans before concerts—do whatever will help your struggle for change to whoever you think can help: the media, the president, the local ROTC, the Elks Club, your grandma, or your old kindergarten teacher. Tell everyone everything all the time. Use the following methods or any others you can think of to enlist support.

What do you enjoy most about your activist work?

Working with other people—brainstorming together and sharing ideas.
—*Robbie Conal, guerrilla postering activist*

No one ever said activism had to be all work all the time. The Pink Bloque incorporates pleasure into our collaborative process as well as our final product. We love to dance, and we use what we love to communicate our messages of social justice. It's a lot of work too, but in order to keep going in discouraging times, we feel it's important to engage fun. Besides, fun is powerful—people don't always respond to negativity. There is fun and pleasure in the world we envision, so why not evoke that now?
—*Blithe (25), The Pink Bloque*

CI suppose the feeling of having a purpose in life, a reason for living. And never being bored!
—*Agent Apple, Biotic Baking Brigade*

reating the spark of passion.
—*Wendy Talley (41), The Spot Youth Center*

Transforming ideas into reality.
—*Joshua Breitbart (29), Allied Media Projects*

What I enjoy most about activist work is the feeling that I am using my time efficiently and effectively, or perhaps the word is effectually. I want to feel that I am participating in my own life. I don't want history to unfold and roll over me. There is not a free and fair exchange of ideas in government or on television news, and I want to work toward changing that.
—*Janeane Garofalo (39), activist, comedian, and actor*

Business letters

Follow the standard business letter format you leaned in school for all communications. Spell all words they way they appear in dictionaries and type your letters (unless you are playing the youth card, in which case you should use crayon and draw a stick-figure picture of yourself at the bottom indicating how happy you will be if they follow through on the request you make in the letter). Choose a single, timely, relevant point for your letter and state it clearly and immediately in the opening sentence. Keep your letter short. Support facts, but do not include too much information. If you are writing to an elected official, write again in a few weeks if you haven't heard back. If you are writing to a media outlet, check every day for two weeks for your letter to appear on TV or in the newspaper before writing again. Convince other people to write letters on the same issue. This will make your issue seem urgent.

Interviews and Debates

If you are asked to give an interview or debate someone, make sure you know your facts. Try to distill everything you want to say into one central message. This is even more important than brushing your hair. If you get nervous or flustered, repeat your central message. If you don't know the answer to a question, say that you don't know. Tell reporters you'll find the answer and get back to them, and then call the reporter back when you find out the answer.

Flyering and Postering

Putting posters up about your cause or event can make you run through staples, tape, and glue very quickly. Wheatpaste, a sturdy poster glue that you can make at home, is another option. It is not always legal to use, because it lasts until the end of time, but I will tell you how to make it anyway, in case you get an art show somewhere or someone donates you a building to plaster. Don't use wheatpaste to put up posters around town, however, because you will undoubtedly be fined, arrested, or embarrassed because your poster will be visible for the rest of your life.

To make wheatpaste you need a pan, flour, water, and a stove. Fill the pan with 1 1/2 cups of water. Dump a cup of flour into the water and stir to get lumps out. Boil and stir this mixture, but don't burn it. You want this goop to thicken and turn clear, and that may take ten or twenty minutes. If it's not turning clear, add small amounts of water until it does. Once the mixture thickens, keep it heated for a few minutes, making sure it doesn't burn. Then dump the goop into a heavy tub. The paste will get thicker as it cools. Use a thick brush to put up your posters. Choose a location, grab your brush, and spread a thick layer of wheatpaste on the wall, about the size of your poster. Place a poster on the paste and brush it down with another layer of wheatpaste, smoothing out any wrinkles. Once your poster is up you will never see what was behind it ever again.

Graphic Design

Posters, flyers, handbills, zines, and informational brochures should all be as cool-looking as possible or they will be ignored. To start any of these projects, ask yourself the purpose of the design and what your creative strengths are. Any artistic skill can be used to create good design. If you are good at copying things off-center or drawing horse heads and cowboy boots, that should be your aesthetic. If you are good at making backwards, lower-case *e*'s in crayon like a little kid, use it to your advantage. Collages, cutout letters, and macaroni glued to paper are all perfect for graphic design. With this in mind, follow these simple steps to design like the pros:

Write out what you need to say. For example, if your fashion show is on the nineteenth from 5 to 11 P.M., don't forget to state it clearly.

Decide what medium you will use (e.g., computer, cut and paste, copier, silkscreen, skywriting). Make sure you know the exact end size of the project and use the space completely. This will make your poster or flyer look professional.

Start putting things together in several different ways. Give yourself choices and plenty of time. Use all your skills. Try new things. Look at things upside down and decide if that makes a stronger statement. In design, the space you *don't* use is as important as the space you *do* use. You can sometimes bring attention and power to your design by taking an element away.

When you have a completed design, evaluate your work. Did you get your message across? Are you satisfied with it? Don't settle for something you don't like. You will always regret it. This is a good opportunity to make sure you have not included anything extraneous. If you have, get rid of it.

Get feedback from friends. Outside input is always useful. Even if your friends have no taste, they will be able to tell you if they understand what you are trying to say. Make changes based on their input.

Keep a good copy for your design portfolio, in case you want someone to hire you to do this kind of job later.

If you are using graphic design techniques to mock an advertising campaign, work directly from a sample of the original. Don't try to remember what it looked like— copy it as directly as possible when laying out your design elements. When you are working in the details later, you will find that it's more important to retain the "feel" of the design, rather than the exact spacing, color, and typographical schemes. Again, use friends' ideas to guide you.

Letterhead and Business Cards

Looking professional comes in handy, so put your name, address, and phone number at the top of a piece of paper in a nice font and send out all your press releases and letters on that. Or, invent a fake organization and use that on your letterhead. Business cards are especially handy for activists. When you meet people at protests you want to work with, you can just hand them cards instead of wasting time digging for a pen.

Press Releases

Use the format below to alert the press of every move you make. Once you have written one good press release, simply slip in the updated information every time something new happens. Then it will be faster to update and send to all the people in Appendix E.

FOR IMMEDIATE RELEASE: These words should appear in the upper left-hand margin, just under your letterhead. Capitalize every letter.

Contact Information: Skip a line or two after release statement and list the name, title, and telephone and fax numbers of you or your spokesperson. List a phone number where you can be reached most of the time.

Headline: Skip two lines after the contact information and use a boldface type. Make this a one-sentence, catchy, active description of your project or event.

Dateline: This should be the city your press release is issued from and the date you are mailing your release ("Austin TX, February 9, 2008," for example).

Lead Paragraph: The first paragraph needs to grab the reader's attention and should contain information relevant to your message such as the five W's (who, what, when, where, and why).

Text: The main body of your press release is where your message should fully develop. Make sure your story is newsworthy, clearly written, and factual. Use the active voice. One or two brief paragraphs should do the trick. Include quotes, even if they're from your little brother. End your final paragraph with the phrase "For additional information, contact:" and then include your contact information. At the very bottom of the page, place three numeral symbols in a row (###). This is journalism lingo for "stop reading now." Try to keep this all on a single page.

Your Project

Now, what will you do? Of course, *you* already know. I'm the one that has no idea. All I can do now is provide you with more information on other sorts of things you may want to know how to do and try. Here you go. Have fun.

Bookbinding and Zine-Making

Making your own book or zine is the only way to exercise true freedom of the press, which is something everyone should experience at least once. Hand-stitch or use a sewing machine to bind paper onto cardboard or a thicker paper surface. You can also drill through paper and tie cord through the drill holes to bind a book, if you can get your hands on a drill. Experiment! If you're planning on writing your own book, incorporate the theme or idea behind your book into your binding ideas. For example, a book about recycling could be made entirely from materials found in your garbage can. The Aktiv Shoes Zine on page 73 shows you a basic zine layout; copy it and experiment with different paper sizes and you should be able to figure out how to make your own. Be sure to keep a copy for yourself and donate a few to your local zine library.

Cable Access

Public access television stations make air-time available to the public for free. Moreover, they often have cheap or free classes that teach you how to shoot, edit, and air a program of your own making. By having your local station air a program, you educate others, build support for your cause, and inspire people to action. You can air a video by a nonprofit organization or produce your own show. To find your local access channels, call your cable com-

effectively with their audiences.
—Jim Keady, Educating for Justice, Inc.

Being able to analyze information and come to their own conclusions.
—Wendy Talley (41), The Spot Youth Center

I wished I had learned more about the history of effective social justice work when I was in middle school and high school. Knowing about movements that actually changed things for the better helps you believe that activism matters and inspires you when things don't seem like they will ever change.
—Dara (32), The Pink Bloque

Learn to turn off the TV.
—The Professor (31), The Infernal Noise Brigade

I think different skills come into play as we need them, and the process of learning is as important as the skills. I wish I had learned earlier how to love myself undefensively and really value my own per-

spective, but of course that was its own journey.
—*Nomy Lamm (28), writer, performer, and community organizer*

I wish I had learned to take care of my health better, instead of just counting on staying young forever!
—*Agent Apple, Biotic Baking Brigade*

Learn the technical skills that you will need to independently get your ideas out (i.e. computer graphics, silk screening, video editing, etc).
—*Rachel (28), The Pink Bloque*

Having love and compassion for all people, even those that are working against you in your work. Always treating them with respect without having to deny your differences, even when they are not respectful. This produces more integrity and respect for the work you are doing.
—*Evon Peter (27), Native Movement*

Keep it simple, stupid!
—*Robbie Conal, guerrilla postering activist*

pany. Not all cable systems allow public access; in fact, many stations owned by companies in Appendix F are trying to replace access channels with more profitable programming.

Community Radio

Several towns still have community radio stations that, like public access television stations, provide classes on editing or recording on their facilities for cheap or free. They may also have slots to volunteer to do production work for an on-air show. Community radio stations are really great, so if you don't have on in your area, you may want to start one.

Copying

No matter what your project is, you will probably have to make copies of something to publicize, distribute, or organize it. Anyone at a copy store (including other customers) can show you how to make copies. If you experiment, you can easily figure out how to come up with a range of neat effects depending on how sophisticated the machine is. Some schools or libraries let kids make free copies. Always be honest about how many you need and what the copies are for, that way you can save the precious space in your brain for more important things than remembering lies. You may want to experiment with silk-screening, potato stamping, or other ways of making multiple copies of one image or text. Don't forget that interesting use of both color and white space (see "Graphic Design," above) can make your project much cooler. It may even be worthwhile to hand-color photocopied covers for your 500 zines.

Duct Tape and Fishing Line

If all else fails, tape it up. If it won't tape, fishing line is the strongest substance known to man. It can be used to fasten, attach, or work

People will tell you to loosen up, ask you why you have to fight all the time, call you naive, say you are too cerebral, wonder why you are wasting your time, tell you this is just the way things are so why bother, and endless other judgments. Know that you are not alone in feeling like you need to stand up. People will judge any path you choose in life, especially if it's going to make waves.
—Natalie (19), The Pink Bloque

Bookkeeping.
—Joshua Breitbart (29), Allied Media Projects

out any problem not resolvable with duct tape. Leaky canoes, broken protest signs, hilarious kidnapping pranks, sculptural creations, quick costumes, loose wires: all this and more can be created or fixed with duct tape and fishing line. Both of these should be kept on hand at all times, like a spare pie.

Holding a Demonstration

The best place to demonstrate is in a location that relates to the problem you want to solve. Choose a convenient time for activists to attend, and a time when employees at the location can observe (mornings or lunch breaks, for example). Plan and organize at least a week in advance, and send press releases and put up fliers immediately. Use your graphic design, sense of humor, repertoire of songs, and interests in theater to create fun, educational opportunities; interesting placards and signs; and smart, new chants and slogans.

Hooking Up a PA

If your project involves speakers, performers, or loud farting noises, a PA system will be helpful to you. A PA system includes a microphone, a mixer, a power amplifier, speakers, and cables. If you want to set up a full PA you will need to rent (many places offer discounts to civic-minded or fundraising projects) or borrow (pay musicians extra) all of these things.

After you have a PA, make sure you know where the stage is going to be and how far it is from the nearest source of power. Try to look at the space beforehand and estimate the lengths of cable you will need. Then, find where the fuse box is located in the venue. Be careful because PAs can blow fuses in houses and smaller, less-prepared venues. After establishing a stage area, figure out where the audience is going to be and decide which direction to set up your speaker so it will evenly project sound to everyone in the space. Prop the main speakers off the ground so they can project above the crowd. Place the speakers about one foot in front of the furthest forward place on stage, parallel to each other to create a smooth sound. Ideally you would like to set the mixing board up at the back of the audience, centered to the stage and speakers. This will give you the best perspective for mixing. If this is not possible, try to make sure you are in front of the speakers so you can hear the sound when making adjustments.

Now connect the mixer, power amp, and speakers (some PAs have a powered mixer that combines power amp and mixing board). Make sure you have all the cables you need for whatever your power amp and speaker require. Find the "Main" outputs from the mixing board. Plug the corresponding cables into the mixing board and connect them to the "Inputs" on the power amp. Next, find the "Outputs" on the power amp and connect cables from the power amp to each speaker. This may require special cables depending on your amp. If you only have one channel to send to two speakers, you can usually daisy-chain the speakers on one channel by attaching one speaker directly to the power amp and the other speaker to the first speaker. If you daisy-chain your speaker to a single channel, don't overwork your amp. Finally, plug everything into the channels on the mixing board. It is important to turn the power on and off in a specific way to avoid harming the speakers: First turn on the mixer, keeping all the mic levels completely off. Second, turn on the power amp. The speakers don't usually require power so you don't need to turn them on. Bring up the main mixer volume slowly, until you get to "0." (This, in audio lingo, is called "unity.") Next, bring up the channel volume that the microphone plugs into. Slowly adjust the mic sensitivity to increase volume. Now ask all the party people in the house to say "hey."

Murals

Murals, big wall paintings, are a popular way to make a point to a community. Plus, politicians love them, because they're great backdrops for baby-kissing photos. Neighborhoods are usually pretty receptive to murals as long as you use pleasing colors, aren't vulgar, and say something generally positive about the community. Sorry, but politicians and civic groups don't seem to appreciate murals about urban kids getting asthma from roach poop or the high rate of domestic abuse in U.S. soldiers' families. Murals have a great and respected history in culture and the arts that extends all the way to current graffiti work. Research it, it's cool.

To make a mural you will need: permission, a wall, an image, paint, brushes, paint-cleaner, and old clothes you don't mind getting dirty. To get permission, find a wall you want to use and ask someone nearby who owns the property. Track the owners down and ask if it's okay to put a mural on their wall. If the owners say no, ask if they have a different wall you could use, or find another wall you like and start over. Come up with the image yourself. Do a bunch of drawings to test stuff out and decide on the colors beforehand so you know what to ask for when requesting donations. Try to get all the supplies donated. (Include copies of your drawings in your proposal.) The trickiest part of a mural is transferring the image to the wall, but it can be easy if you use a slide projector or opaque projector in the dark. Have a painting party with all your friends. Send a press release and invite the mayor or several local business owners. If you make a pie, the local business owners will be receptive to your brilliant ideas about changing their racist hiring policies, and the mayor may grant you a one-on-one meeting to discuss pedestrian-only zones in the city.

Organize a Speaking Event

Having guest speakers attend meetings, demonstrations, film screenings, art shows, or other speaking events is a good way to educate people and inspire activism. Speakers also help spread awareness, raise funds, create publicity, and build grassroots activism campaigns. Many organizations have speakers' bureaus and are willing to send someone out to talk on a particular subject; many schools, libraries, and other facilities have budgets that allow the presenters to get paid. If you have friends in other parts of town that do amazing activist work, maybe bringing them in to speak to your school or neighborhood would be a good place to start. The most important thing in organizing a speaking gig is getting an audience. Get the word out!

Papier maché

Everyone's made papier maché before: just mix flour and water into a gooey paste and draw strips of newspaper through it to create big but light objects and structures. Use balloons like you did in grade school or build a larger framework with duct tape, fishing wire, sticks, and crumpled newspaper. Make puppets, funny hats, or humungous dioramas that illustrate what your neighborhood would look like after nuclear winter sets in.

Planning a Boycott

Don't enter into boycotts lightly; if you are making a public statement against a certain store or purchasable good, you have to be willing to be vocal and public about it. To be effective, enlist others to your cause. It can be difficult to get others to join a boycott because many feel that they are ineffective in a free-market economy. If boycotting is important to you, make sure you research before you plan demonstrations and informational campaigns in order to educate others thoroughly. After you've started a boycott, never, ever support that business or product again until they meet all your demands for change.

Sewing

Not only is it good to know how to sew so you can repair and make your own clothes and create new fashions for your friends, but sewing can be helpful in making things like books and in giving people stitches (if you ever need to do that). The basic principle is simple: thread a sewing needle, tie it off at the end, and bind two pieces of fabric, paper, or skin together. When it is all bound together tie it off again. Everything else is practice and technology. Get an old sewing machine at a thrift store or garage sale and learn how to use it. Sew black armbands for your friends and family if a person or bill you respect and admire dies, or sew yourself a ridiculous costume to wear while marching in the demonstration Princesses and Pirates for Peace.

Stapling

When preparing to make zines, spend thirty bucks on a long-arm stapler from an office supply store—it will be worth it. Get the money or the stapler donated. To put up posters and flyers, buy a solid staple gun. Don't mess around with your activist toolkit. It's important for you to be able to say what you want to say, so invest in good stuff that will last.

Stencils

Cutting designs out of stiff paper and pushing paint through the leftover openings is a very popular activist technique. Experiment with designs, language, images, paint techniques, stains (berry juice applied with a sponge gives a nice subtle look, although it is hard to control), or whatever else you can think of. Stenciling in certain locations is a crime, so get permission or stencil exclusively on T-shirts. In cities with large gang populations, spray paint may no longer be available, so you will have to experiment with stenciling techniques or purchase spray paint online.

Volunteering

Working at an organization is a great way to learn about a specific issue or problem, but don't delude yourself into thinking that volunteering will change the world. The fact that people need to be asked to give their time to volunteer in this country is a symbol that something is terribly wrong. What you change by volunteering is the workload of an organization. If you believe strongly in the mission of an organization, and want to learn from the people there, these are good reasons to volunteer. Try to volunteer with the explicit aim to eliminate the need for all future volunteers. You won't accomplish this goal, but at least you won't be volunteering for the wrong reasons. And in the meantime, you'll learn a lot about an issue that matters to you and meet a ton of experts in your area of activism.

Appendix A

Print Magazines and Reports

A Matter of Time: Risk and Opportunity in the Nonschool Hours. Report on the Task Force on Youth Development and Community Programs. New York: Carnegie Corporation, 1992. A study of how the disappearance of after-school programs impacts kids.

Adbusters. An expensive, pretty magazine with a slick design but debatable activist strategies. (See Adrian Hardy, "Presto," *Adbusters* 44, November/December 2002. A teeny little story about a dance club Nike tried to open to launch a new line of shoes and how the target audience reacted.)

Advertising Age. A regular monthly report on the latest ad techniques and trends by marketers, advertisers, and PR people.

Adweek. Made for advertising executives, *Adweek* offer no-holds barred advice on getting money from little kids.

American Demographics. A bimonthly magazine relaying up-to-the-minute research on what people buy and why.

Bitch. A print magazine with short, snappy articles devoted to feminist commentary on our media-driven world. Because it is published by an always-struggling, not-for-profit corporation, a subscription to this magazine is a good, solid investment in alternative media.

Blackgirl Magazine. Founded by thirteen-year-old Atlanta resident Kenya Jordana James in 2001, this magazine and its youthful staff provide information that entertains and empowers. *Blackgirl* focuses on promoting positive messages and imagery of African American teens, but also provides history, culture, lifestyle, and entertainment news.

Columbia Journalism Review (CJR). The self-proclaimed "Premier Media Monitor" in the U.S. usually features in-depth stories about journalistic trends and the conglomeration of big media.

Clamor. A good source of information and a great place for underground writers and youth to publish political writing.

Consumer Reports. Attempts to accurately inform people about products through extensive research and testing. They aim to be unbiased in their advice and are surprisingly successful.

Extra! This bimonthly magazine from Fairness and Accuracy in Reporting (FAIR) gives regular coverage to untruthful stories covered and spread by the media. Offers fantastic, easy-to-read analysis of specific lies perpetrated by individual reporters, programs, channels, or publications.

Fierce. A feminist magazine out of Atlanta for women from multicultural, diverse viewpoints. Written with a great energy young women will really like and young men will learn from.

In These Times. Investigative journalism and sharp cultural criticism. Not very many illustrations, but good, solid writing and reporting.

Left Turn. A text-heavy independent publication made by and for activists; a great place to find ideas and like-minded people.

Mother Jones. An independent nonprofit magazine with a focus on social justice implemented through investigative reporting. Written by adults for adults (even though Mother Jones was a children's rights advocate), but keep an eye on it anyway.

New Moon: The Magazine for Girls and Their Dreams. A magazine for every girl who wants her voice heard and her dreams taken seriously and for every adult who cares about girls. No makeup tips!

Punk Planet. A fantastic arts-as-activism guide, although heavily weighted toward music. I write for them occasionally, but just 'cause you're sick of me, don't let that stop you from reading this magazine.

Stay Free! Check out their website, but the print version is worth buying whenever it gets printed, which is not very often. This is an irregularly-published, anti-corporate, very unique zine you should really read.

The Nation. A great magazine, although it might be better for older readers who already enjoy reading political journalism. Very text-heavy. (See Marc Cooper, "The Boys and Girls of (Union) Summer," *Nation*, August 12/19, 1996, 18–20, for a look at some of the young people that reenergized unions in the mid-1990s. Also see Jonah Peretti, "My Nike Media Adventure," *Nation*, April 9, 2001.)

The Progressive. A journalistic voice for peace and social justice at home and abroad with a fascinating history of troublemaking.

Appendix B

Books

Abdul-Matin, Ibrahim, Manuela Arcinegas, Pablo Caraballo, Mathilda de Dios, Jee Kim and Kohi Taha, eds. *Future500: Youth Organizing and Activism in the United States*. Chicago: Subway & Elevated Press, 2002. Offers lists of organizations that work with youth as well as descriptions of their work and contact information.

Amidei, Nancy. *So You Want to Make a Difference: Advocacy is the Key!* 14th ed. Washington, DC: OMB Watch, 2002. A book published by nonprofit research and advocacy organization OMB Watch, this guidebook provides all the tools you need to use your government effectively.

Anderson, M.T. *Burger Wuss*. Cambridge: Candlewick Press, 1999. This young adult novel takes a satirical look at consumerism, youth culture, and the fast food industry.

Anonymous. *Pie Any Means Necessary: The Biotic Baking Brigade Cookbook*. Oakland, CA: AK Press, 2004. A documentation and exploration of the Global Pastry Uprising. With recipes!

Bagdikian, Ben H. *The Media Monopoly*. Boston: Beacon Press, 2000. A reference book on corporate media ownership.

Day, Nancy. *Advertising: Information or Manipulation*. Berkeley Heights, New Jersey: Enslow Publishers, 1999. A pretty good, but not very critical, book written for teens providing lots of information about advertising and the history of public relations.

Douglas, Susan J. *Where the Girls Are: Growing Up Female with the Mass Media*. New York: Random House, 1994. A cutesy book written for baby boomers that will give teens the understanding that everyone has been manipulated by the media.

Featherstone, Liza and United Students Against Sweatshops. *Students Against Sweatshops*. New York: Verso, 2002. Documentation of a college student uprising throughout the U.S. that led to changes in labor policies.

Fox, Roy F. *Harvesting Minds: How TV Commercials Control Kids*. Westport, CT: Praeger, 1996. Foreword by George Gerbner. A great, but repetitive, book about how Channel One controls kids' lives.

Gay, Kathlyn. *Caution! This May Be an Advertisement: A Teen Guide to Advertising*. New York: Franklin Watts, 1992. A good beginners' look at advertising tricks.

Hoffman, Abbie. *Steal This Book*. New York: Four Walls Eight Windows, 2002. A funny how-to guide published in the 1970s, this book offers advice on revolting against the consumerist culture. It has been published several times by different companies and is difficult to find in libraries because people keep stealing copies! Look for it anyway.

hooks, bell. *Feminism Is for Everybody*. New York: South End Press, 2000. Recommended by the Pink Bloque, educator bell hooks makes women's rights accessible and interesting.

Klein, Naomi. *No Logo*. New York: Picador USA, 2000. A long book that describes current political activity (mostly based around increased private ownership of public space) and changes that have come about because of these actions.

Lee, Martin A. and Normon Solomon. *Unreliable Sources: A Guide to Detecting Bias in the News Media*. New York: Carol Publishing Group, 1991. A difficult book that talks about who controls the news and how.

Lewis, Barbara. *The Kid's Guide to Social Action*. 2d ed. Minneapolis: Free Spirit Publishing, 1998. A great book about young adults' influence over electoral politics.

Postman, Neil. *Amusing Ourselves to Death: Public Discourse in the Age of Show Business*. New York: Penguin Books, 1985. This is a great book about how TV makes us stupid and boring, and how that is beginning to change our political landscape. Also: *Conscientious Objections:*

Stirring Up Trouble About Language, Technology, and Education. New York: Knopf, 1988. Funny essays and interesting ideas about how language controls politics.

Postman, Neil and Charles Weingartner. *Teaching as a Subversive Activity*. New York: Delta, 1971. Written for kids who want to change education from inside the school.

Postman, Neil and Steve Powers. *How to Watch TV News*. New York: Penguin, 1992. Written by an academic and a news producer, this book is an indispensable guide to understanding television news.

Savan, Leslie. *The Sponsored Life: Ads, TV, and American Culture*. Philadelphia: Temple University Press, 1994. Short, witty columns (reprinted from the *Village Voice*) about the inescapability of contact with corporate money.

Stauber, John and Sheldon Rampton. *Toxic Sludge is Good For You: Lies, Damn Lies and the Public Relations Industry*. Monroe, Maine: Common Courage Press, 1995. Also: *Trust Us, We're Experts!* Monroe, Maine: Common Courage Press, 2001. Two great books that trace the history of PR (and some of the industry's dirtiest tricks) from their humble beginnings.

Wallace, Shelagh. *The TV Book: Talking Back to Your TV*. Toronto: Annick Press, 1998. Activities by Chris M. Worsnop. A great book for kids about how TV shows get made and why you should do more than simply "watch" them.

Williams, Rob. *The Ad and the Ego Curriculum Guide*. San Francisco, 1997. Edited by Chris M. Worsnop, created as a supplement to *The Ad and the Ego*, a video by Harold Boihem. An excellent resource used in conjunction with, or totally separate from, the video (which itself is an excellent starting point for discussions of media influence).

Wimsatt, William Upski. *Bomb the Suburbs*. New York: Soft Skull Press, 1994. Hip-hop activism and tons of great ideas, also from this book's publisher.

Zinn, Howard. *A People's History of the United States*. New York: Harper Perennial, 2003. A different kind of history book.

Appendix C

Websites

Here are some sites that will help you start researching some of the people, projects, and ideas listed in this book.

Aap.org. Research studies and educational materials for families and teachers from the American Academy of Pediatrics.

About-face.org. A cool site about girls' body image and media.

Aclu.org. The ACLU (American Civil Liberties Union) has a section devoted to constitutional violations of students' rights.

Adage.com. The online version of *Advertising Age*.

Adbusters.org. Adbusters' website and culture-jamming resource center.

Agp.org. The site of Peoples' Global Action is a network for spreading information and coordinating actions between grassroots movements around the world.

Airamericaradio.com. Online information about the progressive radio station.

Alliedmediaprojects.org. Find out more about Allied Media Projects, *Clamor*, and the Allied Media Conference in Bowling Green, OH (where you can bring your zines to sell or trade!), an almost ridiculously ambitious yet successful collection of projects.

Alternet.org. A database of alternative and analytical news.

Asfar.org. An organization dedicated to protecting and advancing the legal civil rights of youth, ASFAR (Americans for a Society Free from Age Restrictions) fights the voting age, curfew laws, and other laws that limit young people's freedom.

Asu.edu. The site of the Education Policy Research Unit acts as a watchdog on schools, curricula, and corporate involvement in education.

Billboardliberation.com. This website describes activities and some projects of the Billboard Liberation Front.

Bioticbakingbrigade.org. More information on the Biotic Baking Brigade's pie politics can be found at this site.

Childrennow.org. Contains information on how recent FCC changes affect youth television programming.

Coloredgirls.org. The website of the Women of Color Resource Center is an important resource for anything related to girls' rights.

Commondreams.org. Alternative news and information.

Consumersunion.org. Special reports on consumerism, especially that designed for kids.

Ecommercetimes.com/perl/story/4029.html. Read "Report: Kids Click Webs Ads Most," by Gary Gately, August 15, 2000, for information on how kids view the web.

Educatingforjustice.org. Through educational programming and materials, Jim Keady's Educating for Justice seeks to raise awareness about issues of justice and spark social change.

Fair.org. The website for Fairness and Accuracy in Reporting (FAIR) contains extensive how-to lists and tips for dealing with the media.

Freechild.org. Lists grants and awards for youth activism.

Freespeech.org. This site contains a wide selection of independently produced video and audio projects.

Future500.com. A comprehensive database of youth activism and organizing in the U.S.

Geocities.com/Hollywood/Hills/1902. A video teacher has put her entire nine-week video production curriculum on the web! Includes desktop publishing and video. Daily lesson plans and classroom handouts. Get your teacher to check it out.

Hclib.org. The Hennepin County Library system offers four ways to get your questions answered by librarians: live chat, email, phone, and in-person. When you can't visit Minneapolis, Minnesota's great libraries, email their librarians for advice.

Hierarchies.org. An interactive site where users can look up—and post—corporate ties to consumer products.

House.gov/house/memberwww.html. Addresses and names of members of the House of Representatives.

Highschoolalt.org. Your independent guide to education off the beaten path in the state of Minnesota, written by a girl who didn't feel like high school was for her.

Infernalnoise.org. The Infernal Noise Brigade is loud and fun. Videos and further information are available on its site.

Ideafund.takingitglobal.org. The Ideafund connects innovative ideas with the mentors, knowledge, partners, and funds to transform them into actionable plans.

Iwfr.org. The official site of the Immigrant Workers Freedom Ride provides images, information, and news on current immigration issues.

Jbcc.Harvard.edu/media2/press_seipp.htm. Read "KIDS: The New Captive Audience" for information on how kids are targeted by advertisers, reprinted from *Child Magazine* by Catherine Seipp, September 2001.

Kqed.org/cell/mediaeducation/mediaclassroom/videprodclass. This site offers a resource guide for video production in the classroom, which includes books, magazines, and videos. Also details basic equipment needed for classroom video production.

Mediaandwomen.org. An activist site for feminist media activists and girl activists interested in women's and girls' rights.

Media-awareness.ca. This Canadian site has fantastic ideas to critically engage youth with the media.

Mediaed.org. The Media Education Foundation produces and distributes video documentaries to encourage critical thinking and debate about the relationship between media ownership, commercial media content, and the democratic demand for free flows of information, diverse representations of ideas and people, and informed citizen participation.

Mediarights.org. A nonprofit organization that helps media makers, educators, librarians, nonprofits, and activists use documentaries to encourage action and dialogue on contemporary issues.

Mediaspace.org/MMI/mmi_frame.html. Shows how a handful of corporations dominate the commercial media system.

Nativemovement.org. Native Movement is a nonprofit organization dedicated to grassroots awareness, action, and advocacy on Native Peoples' issues.

Negativland.com. Offers information on copyright law and samples of the group's brilliant and hilarious music, art, and jokes.

Newsreel.org. California Newsreel's website offers Patricia Aufderheide's important essay "General Principles in Media Literacy" online as well as numerous investigative and educational videos appropriate for classroom or home use.

Nlg.org. The National Lawyers Guild is dedicated to the need for basic change in the structure of our political and economic system. The guild unites lawyers, law students, and legal workers as an effective political and social force in the service of the people.

Nomylamm.com. Find out more about performer and activist Nomy Lamm's radical creative work at her website.

Ombwatch.org. OMB Watch provides technical information and assistance to advocates and activists about governmental budgets and accountability. Order Nancy Amidei's *So You Want to Make a Difference* here.

Peta.org. Get involved in animal rights activism. (They even have a youth section on their site!)

Pinkbloque.org. The Chicago-based radical feminist street dance troupe does choreographed and spontaneous dance actions to bring attention to a variety of social justice issues. They have acted against war, the Patriot Act, FCC deregulation, date rape, domestic violence, and are now working on reproductive freedoms.

Prwatch.org/cgi/spin.cgi. Get the latest from the world of public relations professionals in this watchdog report, PR Watch—Spin of the Day.

Reclaimthestreets.net. Provides links to international protests, actions, and street-reclaiming events.

Revbilly.com. The website of Reverend Billy and the Church of Stop Shopping.

Robbieconal.com. Tips on guerilla etiquette and postering from Robbie Conal.

Schoolcommercialism.org. See: Alex Molnar, "Corporate Involvement in Schools: Time For A More Critical Look" from the Center for the Analysis of Commercialism in Education (Winter, 2001). See also: asu.edu, above.

Senate.gov/general/contact_information/senators_cfm.cfm. Addresses and names of senators.

Stayfreemagazine.org. Easier to find than the print version, and most contents of back issues can be found online.

Takebackthemedia.com. Lists links to current corporations' media holdings and provides activist information.

Theonion.com. More "alternative" news and information. By "alternative," I mean fake.

Thepeachclub.org. The PEACH Club, an arts and mentorship program in Chicago, is an innovative model for youth programming and community involvement. Contact and some programming information can be found at this site.

Thespot.org. The Spot Youth Center in Denver, Colorado, provides a safe, supportive space that encourages respect, creativity, education, employment, and career development to at-risk urban youth.

Tolerance.org. The "Mix It Up" section of the website of the Southern Poverty Law Center offers tips and grants for activist teens.

Usasnet.org. The site of United Students Against Sweatshops.

Whitehouse.gov. The president of the United States of America's house.

Witness.org. This group uses video and technology to fight for human rights. Provides access (and links) to some great videos.

Youthactivism.org. A youth advocacy organization, this site offers ideas on convincing community and government leaders that young people must no longer be shut out of decision-making processes and urges organizations and institutions to take seriously the ideas and solutions offered by youth.

Zillions.org. Consumer Reports' *Zillions* magazine (now only online) contains consumer information for kids and research studies about kids and advertising.

Appendix D

Videos

The Ad and the Ego. Parallax Pictures: Harold Boihem, 1997. One of the most provocative films ever made about advertising's impact on individuals and our culture. A must for media studies, civics, communications, public health, social studies, history, and production classrooms.

Affluenza. PBS: 1997. This PBS series deals with the social and environmental costs of materialism. The teacher's guide is full of activities to complement the film.

Mickey Mouse Monopoly. ArtMedia: Chyng Sun and Miguel Picker, 2001. Exploring the connections among Disney, childhood, and corporate power, this Media Education Foundation film takes viewers behind the scenes of the world's most popular family-oriented media conglomerate to explore how children's culture is commercialized. Eye-opening resource for kids, parents, families, and schools alike.

What a Girl Wants. CHC Productions: Elizabeth Massie, 2001. This Media Education Foundation film scrutinizes notions of "femininity" as portrayed in popular media.

Killing Us Softly 3. Jean Kilbourne and Sut Jhally, 2000. Pioneering activist Jean Kilbourne explores images of women in advertising in this funny and provocative film.

Sonic Outlaws. Craig Baldwin, 1995. An excellent documentary describing the legal and ethical issues involved in appropriating media.

Culture Jam. Right to Jam Productions. Lynn Booth and Jill Sharpe, 2001. A documentary that explores culture jammers and artistic activism.

Appendix E

Addresses

If you go ahead and straight up ask most of the people below to make a change to their corporation, they will send you a form letter and include publicity for their company. This can be funny, especially if they thank you for your input, ignore your request, and send you coupons for the product you are asking them to stop manufacturing. However, sometimes it's a good idea to ask anyway. If you have a good project, be creative about whom you ask for help. Write letters to people to borrow space for a concert or art show, to donate software or equipment or food, or to attend your protest or performance. Send them your zines or your radical postcards. If you are nice, people will probably be nice back. Research organizations on their websites, and use standard business letter protocol when writing them. Write a personal letter to the chairwoman or chairman of the board, the senior manager, or the board of directors. It's good business for them to personally respond to you. Even if they hate your ideas, they might learn something by reading what you have to say.

If you write any letters to members of the media, send a copy to FAIR (Fairness and Accuracy in Reporting) so they can stay informed of what the public thinks and does about the media:

FAIR
112 West 27th Street
New York, NY 10001
Email: fair@fair.org

There are far too many government offices to list here, so we'll just put info for the big one:

The President of the United States
1600 Pennsylvania Avenue, NW
Washington, DC 20500
Phone: 202/456-1414
Fax: 202/456-2461
Email: president@whitehouse.gov

Addresses for other local, state, and federal government offices are listed at the front of the phone book.

Write to individual television programs or radio shows, or to specific journalists or DJs in care of (c/o) the station on which the shows are broadcast.

ABC

7 Lincoln Square
New York, NY 10023
Phone: 212/456-7777
OR:
47 West 66th Street
New York, NY 10023
Email: netaudr@abc.com

Associated Press

50 Rockefeller Plaza
New York, NY 10020
Phone: 212/621-1500
Fax: 212/621-7523
Email: info@ap.org

Bertelsmann AG

Carl-Bertelsmann-Straße 270
33311 Gütersloh
Germany
Phone: ++49.5241.80-0
Fax: ++49.5241.80-9662
Email: info@bertelsmann.com

CBS Audience Services

51 West 52nd Street
New York, NY 10019
OR:
CBS News
524 West 57th Street
New York, NY 10019
Phone: 212/975-4321
Fax: 212/975-1893

CNBC

2200 Fletcher Avenue
Fort Lee, NJ 07024
Phone: 201/585-2622
Fax: 201/583-5453
Email: info@cnbc.com

CNN

One CNN Center
POB 105366
Atlanta, GA 30303-5366
Phone: 404/827-1500
Fax: 404/827-1906

Child Labor Coalition
c/o National Consumers League
1701 K Street NW #1200
Washington, DC 20006
Phone: 202/835-3323
Fax: 202/835-0747

Clear Channel Communications
200 East Basse
San Antonio, TX 78209
Phone: 210/822-2828
Fax: 210/822-2299

Columbia Pictures Entertainment Company (Sony)
10202 West Washington Boulevard
Culver City, CA 90232
Phone: 310/280-8000

Dow Jones
Dow Jones & Company
Corporate Headquarters
World Financial Center
200 Liberty Street
New York, NY 10281
Phone: 212/416-2000

Federal Communications Commission
Mass Media Complaints
Chief of Complaints
1919 M Street NW
Washington, DC 20554

Fox Broadcast Studios
POB 900
Beverly Hills, CA 90213
Phone: 310/277-2211

Gannett
Gannett Co., Inc. Headquarters
7950 Jones Branch Drive
McLean, VA 22107
Phone: 703/854-6000

Kellogg Company
One Kellogg Square, POB 3599
Battle Creek, Michigan 49016
Phone: 616/961-2000

Liberty Media Corporation
Liberty Media
9197 South Peoria Street
Englewood, CO 80112
Phone: 720/875-5400
Fax: 720/875-7469

MGM Communications Co.
2500 Broadway
Santa Monica, CA 90404-3061
Phone: 310/449-3000

NBC Entertainment
President
30 Rockefeller Plaza
New York, NY 10020

NPR
635 Massachusetts Avenue NW
Washington, DC 20001-3753
Phone: 202/513-2000
Fax: 202/513-3329
Email: ombudsman@npr.org

Nabisco
CEO: Stephen Goldstone
1301 Avenue of the Americas
New York, NY 10019
OR:
Nabisco Consumer Affairs
100 DeForest Avenue, POB 1911
East Hanover, NJ 07936-1911
Phone: 800/622-4726

News Corp.
Corporate Headquarters
10000 Santa Monica Boulevard
Los Angeles, CA 90067
Phone: 310/369-7540

Nickelodeon
1515 Broadway
New York, NY 10036
212/258-7579

Nintendo of America, Inc.
Corporate Communication Manager
4820 150th Avenue NE
Redmond, WA 98052
Phone: 206/882-2040

PBS
1320 Braddock Place
Alexandria, VA 22314
Phone: 703/739-5000
Fax: 703/739-8458

RJR Tobacco Company
401 North Main Street
Winston Salem, NC 27102
OR:
RJR Tobacco Company
Advertising Dept., POB 7
Winston Salem, NC 27102
Phone: 800/334-8157

Sega of America
Consumer Services 240 D
Shoreline Drive
Redwood City, CA 94065
Phone: 415/802-1338

Time Warner Entertainment Company
75 Rockefeller Plaza
New York, NY 10019
Phone: 212/484-8000
Fax: 212/333-3987

Twentieth Century-Fox Film
10201 West Pico Boulevard
Los Angeles, CA 90035
Phone: 310/369-2211

USA Today
7950 Jones Branch Drive
McLean, VA 22108
Phone: 800/872-0001
Fax: 703/854-2165
Email: editor@usatoday.com

United Press International
1510 H Street NW
Washington, DC 20005
Phone: 202/898.8000
Fax: 202/898.8057
Email: tips@upi.com

Universal Pictures
100 University City Plaza
Universal City, CA 91608
Phone: 818/777-1000

Wall Street Journal
200 Liberty Street
New York, NY 10281
Phone: 212/416-2000
Fax: 212/416-2658
Email: wsj.ltrs@wsj.com

Walt Disney Company
500 South Buena Vista Street
Burbank, CA 91501
Phone: 818/560-1000

Warner Brothers, Inc.
4000 Warner Boulevard
Burbank, CA 91522
Phone: 818/954-6000

Washington Post
1150 15th Street NW
Washington, DC 20071
Phone: 202/334-6000
Fax: 202/334-5269
Email: letters@washpost.com
OR: ombudsman@washpost.com

Appendix F

Big Media

Much of what you see, hear, and do in any given day is influenced by one of the companies listed below. Although media companies change hands fast these days, this chart will give you a place to start researching who owns what.

Product/Service	Corporate Division
Partial owner of News Corporation (see below)	Other media giants
Shares properties with Time Warner (see below)	
Cell-phones Local and long-distance phone services	Telephones
Laurel Leaf Paperback [Lloyd Alexander, Annette Curtis Klause, Chris Crutcher, Philip Pullman] Pantheon	Random House Publishing (a partial list; Random House was chosen by Borders to select content for display in all Borders' children's sections)
YM	Magazines (a partial list)
Arista Records [Kelis, Pink, Outkast] RCA Records [Christina Aguilera, Kelly Clarkson, The Strokes]	BMG music labels (a partial list)
KBCO, KBPI, KHIH, KHOW, KOA, KRFZ, KTCL, and KTLK (all in Denver, CO) KALL, KKAT, KNRS, KODJ, KURR, KWLW, and KZHT (all in Salt Lake City, UT) WGAR, WMJI, WMMS, WMVX, and WTAM (all in Cleveland, OH) KZRR, KPEK, KTEG, KLSK, and KSYU (all in Albuquerque, NM) WALC, WEZL, WRFQ, WSCC, and WXYL (all in Charleston, SC)	Radio (a partial list of the over 1,200 stations owned by Clear Channel throughout the U.S.; listing does not include TV or entertainment venues also owned by Clear Channel)

Consumers	Parent Company
(see below)	**AT&T Corporation** A member of what Mark Crispin Miller called "The media cartel that keeps us fully entertained and permanently half-informed," in the January 8, 2002, *Nation*.
Over 70 million U.S. customers, possibly including you	
Students, readers, young adult and adult book fans, including you	**Bertelsmann AG** The world's largest publisher, Bertelsmann helped the SS print Nazi material during the Third Reich, according to the independent historical commission for investigating the history of Bertelsmann (from uhkommission.de).
Young women magazine readers (maybe you)	
Music fans like you	
A vast majority of the radio-listening public in these and virtually every other area of the United States, more than likely including you	**Clear Channel Communications** The CEO of Clear Channel (with more than 1,200 stations) told *Fortune* magazine in March 2003: "If anyone said we were in the radio business, it wouldn't be someone from our company. We're not in the business of providing news and information. We're not in the business of providing well-researched music. We're simply in the business of selling our customers products."

Product/Service	Corporate Division
KDDK, KMJX, KOLL, KQAR, and KSSN (all in Little Rock, AK) FFGO, WDAY, KVOX, KULW, and KRVI (all in Fargo, ND) WHO, KKDM, KLYF, KMXD, KCCQ, and KASI (all in Des Moines, IA) WENN, WERC, WMJJ, WDXB, and WQEN (all in Birmingham, AL) KATZ, KLOU, KMJM, KSD, and KSLZ (all in St. Louis, MO) WDOV, WDSD, WJBR, and WRDX (all in Wilmington, DE) KTLK, KEX, KKCW, KKRZ, and KRVO (all in Portland, OR) WHAS, WAMZ, WQMF, WTFX, WWKY, WKJK- AM, WYBL, and WZTR (all in Louisville, KY) KFMS, KQOL, KSNE, and KWNR (all in Las Vegas, NV) KBEC, KJYO, KQSR, KTOK, KTST, KXXY, and WKY (all in Oklahoma City, OK) WATQ, WBIZ, WMEQ, and WQRB (all in Eau Claire, WI) WCOH, WGSE, WGST, WKLS, WMAX, WMKJ, and WPCH (all in Atlanta, GA) WFSJ, WJBT, WJGR, WNZS, WPLA, WQIK, WROO, WSOL, and WZNZ (all in Jacksonville, FL) WBGG, WDVE, WJJJ, WKST, WWSW, and WXDX (all in Pittsburgh, PA) KARO, KCIX, KFXD, KIDO, KLTB, and KXLT (all in Boise, ID) KASH, KBFX, KENI, KGOT, KTZN, and KYMG (all in Anchorage, AK)	Radio

Consumers	Parent Company
	Clear Channel Communications

Product/Service	Corporate Division
WGUY, WVOM, WBYA, WBFB, WKSQ, and WLKE (all in Bangor, ME) WJMN, WKOX, WXKS, and WXKS (all in Boston, MA) KFNK, KHHO, KJR, and KUBE (all in Seattle, WA) WCPV, WEAV, WEZF, WJVT, and WXZO (all in Burlington, VT)	Radio
USA Today *Honolulu Advertiser* (in Hawaii) *Layfayette Journal and Courier, Marion Chronicle-Tribune, Richmond Palladium-Item, Indianapolis Star*, and *Muncie Star-Press* (all in Indiana) *Monroe News-Star, Shreveport Times, Alexandria Town Talk, Opelousas Daily World, Lafayette Daily Advertiser* (all in Louisiana) *Asbury Park Press, Bridgewater Courier-News, Cherry Hill Courier-Post, East Brunswick Home News Tribune, Morristown Daily Record, Vineland Daily Journal* (all in New Jersey)	Newspapers (a partial list)
Air Force Times *Army Times* *Defense News* *Navy Times* *Navy Times Marine Corps*	Army Times Publishing Company (a partial list)

Consumers	Parent Company
	Clear Channel Communications
Almost everyone in the U.S. who reads news-papers, probably including your parents, your friends' parents and maybe even you	Gannett The "Game Plan" of this company—circula-tion-wise, the largest U.S. distributor of newspapers—according to gannett.com: "Gannett is an international, multi-billion dollar news, information and communica-tions company that delivers quality products and results for its readers, viewers, advertis-ers and other customers. We believe that well-managed newspapers, television sta-tions, Internet products, magazine/specialty publications and programming efforts will lead to higher profits for our shareholders."
Military personnel (perhaps you or your family), people affected by the military (everyone)	

Product/Service	Corporate Division
Cincinnati Reds (partial owner)	Sports
Bravo! CNBC Independent Film Channel NBC Telemundo	Cable and television
Jet engines and gas turbines	GE Aircraft Engines
Credit	GE Consumer Finance
Insurance	GE Insurance
Energy	GE Power Systems
Biosolids	GE Specialty Materials
MSNBC	Operated in partnership with Microsoft
Discovery Channel The Learning Channel Animal Planet MacNeil/Lehrer Productions (partial owner)	Television and cable
Sprint PCS Group (partial owner)	Telephones

Consumers	Parent Company
Sports enthusiasts like you and your friends	Gannett
Television audiences of all ages, both English- and Spanish-speaking, probably including you	General Electric "From jet engines to power generation, financial services to plastics, and medical imaging to news and information, GE people worldwide are dedicated to turning imaginative ideas into leading products and services that help solve some of the world's toughest problems," (from the company website, atge.com/en).
The military and people who are effected by the military's actions, like you	
Individuals (adults), creditors, auto dealers, maybe your family	
Adults interested in investment opportunities and the preservation and enhancement of wealth and lifestyles (perhaps your family)	
Energy companies, energy consumers (like you)	
Consumers of fused quartz, polymer additives, silicone, industrial diamond, and water treatment solutions (maybe you)	
People who enjoy news—family, teachers, friends or yourself	
Cable users with interests in science and animals (maybe you)	Liberty Media The "global commercial media system . . . is a disaster for anything but the most superficial notion of democracy," Robert W. McChesny stated in the November/December 1997 *Extra!*
Phone users (maybe you)	

Product/Service	Corporate Division
HarperCollins [Lemony Snickett, Meg Cabot, Louise Rennison] *New York Post* *Sunday Times* (London) *TV Guide* (partial owner)	Publications (a partial list)
20th Century Fox	Film (a partial list)
KRIV and KTXH (in Houston, TX) KUTP and KSAZ (in Phoenix, AZ) WNYW and WWOR (in New York, NY)	Television stations (a partial list)
Fox Broadcasting Company National Geographic Channel Jetix (partially owned with Disney)	Television and cable (a partial list)
LA Dodgers Los Angeles Lakers (partial owner) New York Knickerbockers (partial owner) New York Rangers (partial owner) Staples Center	Sports
Columbia Pictures [*Spider-Man, Spider-Man 2*] Sony Pictures [*The Lost Skeleton of Cadavra, Dragon Tales, Seinfeld, The Steve Harvey Show*] Loews Theaters (partial owner) Columbia [Beyoncé, Bow Wow] Epic [Good Charlotte, Cyndi Lauper, Korn]	Film and television
Columbia House (partial owner)	Music
Play Station	Digital Entertainment

Consumers	Parent Company
Young adult book readers, New York and London residents, news junkies, TV junkies, adult readers, and you	News Corporation "Our reach is unmatched in the world. We're reaching people from the moment they wake up until they fall asleep," Rupert Murdoch boasted in the company's annual report of
Probably, at some point, you	1999.
Residents of these cities who watch television, maybe you, if you like the Simpsons	
Fox Kids, nature lovers, television viewers, etc.; Jetix predicts viewers in 137 million households, 77 countries, and 18 languages	
Sports fans and players (perhaps you and your friends)	
People who rent or attend movies	Sony Explaining why Sony advocated spying on Greenpeace, Friends of the Earth, and other ecological organizations in 2000, Burhan Wazir wrote in the October 1 *London Observer* that "its products contain toxins and are difficult to dispose of. Environmentalists would like tougher controls. Sony wants to avoid them."
Music fans	
Gamers (like you or your friends?)	

Product/Service	Corporate Division
Credit	Finance
Insurance	Insurance
Batteries	Miscellaneous
Play	Nightclub
CNN (and CNN Newsroom) Castle Rock Entertainment Cinemax Comedy Central HBO Hanna-Barbera Cartoons WB Television Network [*Mucha Lucha*] Warner Bros. [the Harry Potter movies]	Film, television, and cable (a partial list)
Children's Book-of-the-Month Club Little, Brown and Company [*Zoey Dean*]	Books (a partial list)
Entertainment Weekly DC Comics [*Superman, Wonder Woman*] *Fortune* *Mad Magazine* *People* *Popular Science* *Ride BMX* *Sports Illustrated*	Magazines and comics (a partial list)

Consumers	Parent Company
Adults	Sony
Adults concerned with the security of their finances and health	
People who purchase Sony products and all other electronic equipment that uses batteries (probably, at some point, you)	
Adults with an interest in playing Play Station games with famous people in a public location where alcohol is served	
Students (in the case of CNN Newsroom), news junkies, and cable customers, almost everyone with access to TV or interested in movies (including fans of Daffy Duck, scary movies, and Scooby Doo)	Time Warner Ben Bagdikian noted in the 2000 edition of *The Media Monopoly* that the U.S. has 7 major film studios, 1000 TV stations, 1700 daily newspapers, 2500 book publishers, 9000 radio stations, and 11,000 mainstream magazines. If each were separately owned and controlled, there would be about 25,000 unique media voices in the U.S. instead of around 50. (From the introduction, Boston: Beacon Press, 2000, p. liv.)
Kids and adults (probably you)	
BMX riders, skateboarders, movie fans, collectors, dental assistants, sports fans, weird adults with no social skills, regular adults, business owners, financial investors, etc., etc.	

Product/Service	Corporate Division
Time *Transworld Skateboarding* Vertigo Comics [*The Witching, 100 Bullets, Hellblazer*]	Magazines and comics (a partial list)
Elektra/Sire [Missy Elliott, Third Eye Blind] Maverick [Alanis Morissette, Madonna] Columbia House	Music (a partial list)
AOL Amazon.com (partial owner) Mapquest.com Netscape Communications	Online Services (a partial list)
TBS Superstation Cartoon Network [*Dexter's Laboratory, Teen Titans*] New Line Cinema	Time Warner Inc.—Turner Entertainment (a partial list)
Atlanta Braves Atlanta Hawks Atlanta Thrashers Good Will Games Philips Arena	Sports Teams
Warner Brothers Recreation Enterprises Six Flags	Theme parks
Hasbro (partial owner) Atari (partial owner)	Toy companies

Consumers	Parent Company
	Time Warner (formerly AOL Time Warner
Music fans likely including you	
Kids and adults with online access, interested in purchasing books or getting directions (AOL has 27 million subscribers and you might be one)	
Cable customers like you or your friends	
Kids, adults, maybe your Uncle Leo	
Kids, adults, families (maybe you)	
Kids. Many, many kids.	

Product/Service	Corporate Division
Paramount Pictures [*School of Rock, Mean Girls*]	Film
BET CBS [*Survivor, The Late Show with David Letterman*] Comedy Central (50% with Time Warner) MTV Nickelodeon [*SpongeBob Squarepants, Rugrats*] Showtime UPN [*Girlfriends, America's Next Top Model, Star Trek: Enterprise*] VH1	Television and cable
Spelling Television	Television production and distribution
Famous Music (owner of over 100,000 copyrights to songs)	Music company
WBLK, WBUF, WECK, WJYE, and WYRK (all in Buffalo, NY) WBAV, WFNZ, WGIV, WNKS, WPEG, WSOC, and WSSS (all in Charlotte, NC) WKRK, WOMC, WVMV, WWJ, WXYT, and WYCD (all in Detroit, MI) KMGV, KMJ, KOOR, KOQO, KRNC, KSKS, and KVSR (all in Fresno, CA)	Radio (a partial list)
Blockbuster Video	Other
Paramount Parks	Theme parks

Consumers	Parent Company
Moviegoers	Viacom
	"You can literally pick an advertiser's needs and market that advertiser across all the demographic profiles, from Nickelodeon with the youngest consumers to CBS with some of the oldest consumers," *Time* reported of Viacom in 2000.
Fans of funny, musical, entertaining, dramatic, melodramatic, socially aware, or popular programming, probably including you	
Fans of Tori Spelling (probably not you)	
Anyone affected by the music business	
People who listen to the radio sometimes or all the time (like you)	
Movie-renting people like you	
People who like theme parks (maybe you)	

Product/Service	Corporate Division
Infinity Outdoor	Advertising (mostly billboards)
Simon and Schuster [*Bob the Builder*, *Peanuts*, Nancy Drew, *Bunnicula*]	Book publishing (a partial list)
Senator John McCain	Elected officials (partial list; Viacom was McCain's fourth largest contributor even before McCain proposed changing U.S. rules regulating media ownership after Viacom had violated them by a purchase of CBS)
Cineplex Odeon Corporation (theater chain, partial owner) October Films (majority interest) United Cinema International Universal Studios [*The Hulk*, *The Cat in the Hat*] USA Network	Film and television production and distribution
Rolling Stone	Publishing (a partial list; owns 60 publishing houses)
Blizzard Entertainment Sierra Sega GameWorks (partial owner)	Games and gaming centers
Def Jam [Ja Rule, Ludacris] Motown [Jackson 5, India.Arie, Erykah Badu, Stevie Wonder]	Music (a partial list)
TicketMaster (partial owner) Universal Concerts (concert promotion) Universal Studios Hollywood	Theme parks and retail

Consumers	Parent Company
People who go outside like you	Viacom
Young adults, students, adults, readers, and most likely, you	
Citizens of the U.S. and others affected by its laws, including you	
People who have watched movies and TV (maybe you?)	Vivendi Universal "The profit whole for the global media giant can be vastly greater than the sum of the media parts. A film, for example, should also generate a soundtrack, a book, and merchandise, and possibly spin-off TV shows, CD-ROMs, video games and amusement park rides. Firms that do not have conglomerated media holdings simply cannot compete in this market." (From Robert W. McChesney's "The Global Media Giants," *Extra!* November/December 1997.)
Rolling Stone readers	
Gamers (maybe you)	
People who listen to music and attend concerts including oldies, popular, classical, blues, and all other kinds (like you)	
Families and kids, concertgoers (you?)	

Product/Service	Corporate Division
Universal's Islands of Adventure Theme Park Wet-n-Wild Orlando Spencer Gifts	Theme parks and retail
Vivendi Environment (world's largest water distributor)	Water
MP3.com	Music download site
Waste and recycling management	Recycling Facilities
ABC [*Recess, The Bachelor, The Big House*] Disney Channel ESPN Jetix (partial owner with News Corporation)	Television and cable stations
Radio Disney WMVP, WLS, WZZN, and WRDZ (all in Chicago, IL) WBAP, KSCS, KMEO, KESN, and KMKI (all in Dallas, TX) KABC, KLOS, KDIS, and KSPN (all in Los Angeles, CA) KQRS, KXXR, KDIZ, WGVX, WGVY, and WGVZ (all in Minneapolis/St. Paul, MN) WMAL, WJZW, and WRQX (all in Washington DC)	Radio stations
Buena Vista Television Touchstone Television	Television production and distribution

Consumers	Parent Company
	Vivendi Universal
Ummm . . . people who drink water	
Music fans with internet access (probably your friends, if not you)	
People who recycle	
Television viewers and cable subscribers like you; Jetix predicts viewers in 137 million households, 77 countries, and 18 languages	The Walt Disney Company Disney is "uniquely positioned to fulfill virtually any marketing option, on any scale, almost anywhere in the world," according to the July 8, 1995, *Advertising Age*. Disney, according to Ben H. Bagdikian in his introduction to *The Media Monopoly*, holds "overwhelming power, not just over the media marketplace but over youth culture in the United States and globally." (Boston: Beacon Press, 2000, p. xx.)
Kids, young adults, adults, music fans, news junkies, and people who listen to talk radio, perhaps you	
People who watch TV shows (probably you)	

Product/Service	Corporate Division
Walt Disney Pictures [*The Lion King*, *Cinderella*, *Home on the Range*] Touchstone Pictures Miramax Films [*Kill Bill*]	Movie production and distribution
Crude petroleum and natural gas (partial owner)	Sid R. Bass
The Disney Store	Retail
Film, TV program, clothing, toy, lunchbox, bed-sheet, tattoo, and artistic use	Licensed Characters
Mr. Showbiz Disney.com NFL.com NBA.com NASCAR.com Toysmart.com (partial owner)	Online
Mighty Ducks of Anaheim	Sports
Disneyland Epcot Magic Kingdom Walt Disney World Disney Cruise Line The Disney Institute	Theme parks and resorts
TiVo (partial owner)	Other
Celebration, FL	Town

Consumers	Parent Company
Movie viewers much like you	The Walt Disney Company
Energy consumers—for example, you	
Shoppers (maybe you)	
All media consumers	
Online researchers, sports fans, NASCAR fans, movie enthusiasts, and people searching for educational toys (maybe someone you know . . . or you?)	
People who like hockey (maybe you)	
Kids, young adults, adults, and elderly people interested in vacationing, relaxing, or learning (at one point, maybe you)	
Parents, sports fans, people who enjoy TV and can afford this product, maybe your family	
Residents and neighbors of this pre-planned town (probably not you)	

Appendix G

Excerpted from
Policy Advocacy: The Ten Minute Version
By Nancy Amidei

Part of OMB Watch's series Tools for Advocates

Advocacy means *to speak up*, *to plead the case of another*, or *to champion a cause*. Usually advocacy involves bringing influence to bear to win change. It is something most of us do routinely on behalf of ourselves, our families, our neighbors, and our friends.

Policy advocacy is no different, except that the advocacy may be on behalf of people we don't personally know, and those being influenced work with laws, public programs, or court decisions. That includes anyone in a public policy-making role (like a county commissioner, state legislator, or government employee).

Policy advocacy can be useful at all levels of government. For example, if you have a family member with a mental or physical disability, policies at federal, state, and local levels already affect your lives:

- Local school boards must carry out the federal law that requires an Individualized Education Plan for handicapped children;
- County government is usually responsible for such social services as sheltered workshops and adult day care;

- City government is likely to be responsible for whether or not buses, roadways, and public buildings are accessible to wheelchairs;
- State government determines the income eligibility limits for Medicaid; and
- The federal government is responsible for protecting the civil rights of people with disabilities.

One way or another, legislators, government agencies and the courts all affect whether people with disabilities and their families can live full and productive lives. But sometimes it takes the help of an advocate to make everything work as it should.

If you want to make a positive difference for vulnerable people in your community, then you will need to take three steps:
1. Be informed. This part is obvious. It doesn't help to be well-meaning but misinformed. Getting the basic facts is the first step, and not very hard.

Get on the mailing list of an advocacy group that focuses on your issue. If you are concerned about the need for child care in your community, you could get to the mailing list of a national or local child advocacy group, and go to public meetings where child care needs are discussed. Local advocates can direct you to reports on the subject, and you could follow the issue in the media. Before long, you'll know a lot about child care.

2. Be involved. This step is also pretty obvious, and one that most people take almost instinctively. It makes sense to want to act once you know the need.

Here too there are many possibilities. You could volunteer at a Head Start program, attend a conference, or answer telephone inquiries at a Resource and Referral line. Others help by babysitting for the children of homeless families while their parents are out looking for housing or work.

Taking steps one and two will help alleviate some immediate problems. That is a good thing, but the problems will still be there, as will their causes—argely unchanged. Just being informed—without acting—is like going to a restaurant just to read the menu. You'd be informed, but you'd be missing the point. To be effective, one more step is needed.

3. Be an advocate. This does not come as easily to most people, but it represents the best hope for getting at why there is a problem in the first place.

Here too there are many choices for action. You could make calls or write letters about child care measures before your state legislature. You could help design and carry out a campaign to educate the voters. You can urge your governor to support adequate child care funding. You can write letters when federal regulations affecting child care are revised. In short, you can take steps to insure that there will be real child care choices available to meet the needs in your community.

Three Basic Tools, Two Critical Audiences

No matter what the level of government, the nature of the change desired, or the need, there are three basic tools available to every policy advocate and two key audiences. When you want to reach a policy maker you should plan to:

Write   Call   Visit

If policy makers are to represent your wishes in the policy process, they need to hear from you. The fundamentals of convincing policy makers are so reasonable you'll wonder why you haven't done it (or more of it) before.

- Be brief and to the point;
- Identify yourself and how you (or people you know) will be affected by what's being proposed - that is, a new law, a cut in the budget, a change in the rules that govern a program;
- Be clear about what you want. Name the law that's being discussed or the program rules that are about to be changed, and specifically what you want the policy-maker to do;
- Mention provisions that you agree and disagree with, and ifpossible, offer some alternative;
- Let them know how you can be reached for further information, a clarification, or help.

In addition to reaching policy makers directly, there's a second audience to keep in mind: other voters. If enough of them get aroused, they will help make your case, and your job will be easier. The same basic tools apply.

Write

With a few minor changes, the letter you sent to a legislator can also be sent as a letter-to-the-editor. That way your message may reach many other voters.

Call

The same message you leave on your Congressperson's message machine can be called into a radio call-in show. That's another way your message can reach other voters.

Visit

Or, you can take the "little speech" you memorized to speak to the county commissioner the other day at the mall, and repeat it at your church group, country club, or PTA. That's one more way that your message can reach other voters.

Basic Advocacy Is Not Hard

While it is certainly true that some advocacy is carried out by experts and may involve super-sophisticated organizations and strategies, there is still much to do that is simple and easy. You don't need to be an expert, you just need to care enough to get involved and speak up. That means bringing whatever power you have—as a taxpayer and a voter—to make our democratic system work. Your influence is greater than you think and not hard to use. Just consider:

- Speaking up won't guarantee that you will win, but not speaking up guarantees that your wishes won't be known.
- Advocacy is easier, and frequently more fun,if you are part of a group. (It also helps booster your courage and bolster morale).
- It helps to go along with someone more experienced the first few times. It won't seem so intimidating and having someone else do the talking helps a lot. Much of learning involves watching (and imitating) others. Advocacy is no different.
- Don't be afraid of being asked something you can't answer. Many politicians have message machines, so you may just be talking to a machine. And, as one Senate aide explained, her job was to record each caller's name, address, and message—not to put the senator's constituents on the spot by interrogating them.
- What if you were asked something you can't answer? Simple, do as the politicians do: say you don't know, but you'll find out and get back to them. Then do. When Utah governor Norman Bangerter met with human needs advocates at a "Citizen's Day At the Legislature," there were questions he

couldn't answer. He acknowledged the fact and said he'd get back to the groups with the answer. You can do the same.

- •Don't be afraid of being rejected. As one politician explained, even if he thought your idea was goofy, he'd fudge around or nod rather than say so. Elected officials are not likely to risk losing your vote by telling you off.
- • Practice helps. Memorize a little speech, or write out a script to use on the phone. Role-play the meeting or call with a friend. And don't worry if you lack the charm of Ronald Reagan or the moral stature of Mother Teresa.

Your only task is to be yourself: a citizen and voter who wants government policies to work for the most vulnerable as well as they do for the most powerful.

Anne Elizabeth Moore has written for the *Onion*, *Punk Planet*, *Clamor*, the *Stranger*, *Bridge*, the *Chicago Reader*, the *Comics Journal*, and the *Progressive*. She holds a master's degree in art history, theory, and criticism from the School of the Art Institute of Chicago and a bachelor of fine arts in photography from the University of Wisconsin. She has lectured across North America (including in-person, radio, and television appearances on CNN, NPR, and various local outlets) on the use of imagery in political popular culture. A long-time self-publisher with over thirty single-shot zines to her credit, Moore has traveled throughout the country addressing issues of independent publishing to audiences of various ages and experiences. She was named Industrial Strength Woman by Friends of Lulu in 2001 (for work in comics) and nominated for two Eisner Awards and two Harvey Awards in 2002 (for work in comics).